UNDERSTANDING SEXUAL VIOLENCE

A Study of Convicted Rapists

Perspectives on Gender, Volume 3

Diana Scully

Boston
UNWIN HYMAN
London   Sydney   Wellington

Barnard

Unwin Hyman, Inc.
955 Massachusetts Avenue, Cambridge, Mass. 02139, USA

Published by the Academic Division of
Unwin Hyman Ltd
15/17 Broadwick Street, London W1V 1FP, UK

Allen & Unwin (Australia) Ltd,
8 Napier Street, North Sydney, NSW 2060, Australia

Allen & Unwin (New Zealand) Ltd in association with the
Port Nicholson Press Ltd,
Compusales Building, 75 Ghuznee Street, Wellington 1, New Zealand

First published in 1990

BARNARD
HV
6561
.S42
1990
C.1

Library of Congress Cataloging in Publication Data

Scully, Diana.
    Understanding sexual violence : a study of convicted rapists /
Diana Scully.
        p. cm. — (Perspectives on gender : v. 3)
    Includes bibliographical references (p.).
    ISBN 0-04-445141-5. — ISBN 0-04-445846-0 (pbk.)
    1. Rape—United States. 2. Rapists—United States—Attitudes.
3. Rape—United States—Public opinion. 4. Public opinion—United
States. I. Title. II. Series.
HV6561.S42 1990
364.1532'0973—dc20   90-12258
                                                               CIP

British Library Cataloguing in Publication Data

Scully, Diana, 1941–
    Understanding sexual violence : a study of convicted
    rapists. – (Perspectives on gender; v.3)
    1. Crimes. Rapes
    I. Title   II. Series
    364.1532

    ISBN 0-04-445141-5
    ISBN 0-04-445846-0   pbk

Typeset in 10/12 point Palatino
Printed in Great Britain by Billings and Sons, Ltd, Worcester

Dedicated to the victims

Understanding
Sexual Violence

PERSPECTIVES ON GENDER

Additional titles in preparation

Barnard

Unwin Hyman, Inc.
955 Massachusetts Avenue, Cambridge, Mass. 02139, USA

Published by the Academic Division of
Unwin Hyman Ltd
15/17 Broadwick Street, London W1V 1FP, UK

Allen & Unwin (Australia) Ltd,
8 Napier Street, North Sydney, NSW 2060, Australia

Allen & Unwin (New Zealand) Ltd in association with the
Port Nicholson Press Ltd,
Compusales Building, 75 Ghuznee Street, Wellington 1, New Zealand

First published in 1990

Library of Congress Cataloging in Publication Data

Scully, Diana.
    Understanding sexual violence : a study of convicted rapists /
Diana Scully.
        p. cm. — (Perspectives on gender : v. 3)
    Includes bibliographical references (p.).
    ISBN 0-04-445141-5. — ISBN 0-04-445846-0 (pbk.)
    1. Rape—United States. 2. Rapists—United States—Attitudes.
3. Rape—United States—Public opinion. 4. Public opinion—United
States. I. Title. II. Series.
HV6561.S42 1990
364.1532'0973—dc20   90-12258
                                                                    CIP

British Library Cataloguing in Publication Data

Scully, Diana, 1941–
    Understanding sexual violence : a study of convicted
    rapists. – (Perspectives on gender; v.3)
    1. Crimes. Rapes
    I. Title   II. Series
    364.1532

    ISBN 0-04-445141-5
    ISBN 0-04-445846-0   pbk

Typeset in 10/12 point Palatino
Printed in Great Britain by Billings and Sons, Ltd, Worcester

UNDERSTANDING SEXUAL VIOLENCE

A Study of Convicted Rapists

Perspectives on Gender, Volume 3

Diana Scully

Boston
UNWIN HYMAN
London   Sydney   Wellington

Contents

CONTENTS

Acknowledgments

In the ten years that I have been working on this project, I have accumulated a debt of gratitude to a long list of individuals and institutions. The National Center for the Prevention and Control of Rape at the National Institute of Mental Health funded the research on convicted rapists. I especially want to thank the exceptional staff of women at the National Center with whom I worked during those years and to acknowledge their feminist foresight. The research could not have been done without the generous cooperation of the Virginia Department of Corrections, the staffs of the seven prisons in which the research took place, and, of course, the men who volunteered to be interviewed. In different ways, I am grateful and indebted to them all.

Joseph Marolla and I collaborated on the development of the NIMH grant, and on the data gathering, analysis, and early writing. His insight and sociological imagination are evident throughout this manuscript, but the interpretations and opinions expressed herein are my own.

I am grateful for the love and support of my family and the encouragement of colleagues at Virginia Commonwealth University. The interest and enthusiasm of my students, too numerous to mention, has been especially important, and, in particular, I am grateful to Diane Berry and Lloyd (Chip) Byrd for their contributions to this project.

Over the years a number of individuals have read parts of the manuscript and made valuable suggestions. I particularly want to thank Margaret Anderson, Pauline Bart, Ann Wolbert Burgess, Rutledge Dennis, David Franks, Norrece Jones, Judith Lorber, Neil Henry, James Orcutt, and Malcolm Spector. Lisa Freeman, my editor at Unwin Hyman, and Myra Marx Ferree provided the essential urging that got this book completed, and I thank them for their infectious enthusiasm. Finally, I am grateful for the intellectual stimulation and nurturance of the many feminist scholars whose work broke the ground for this book.

Some of the ideas contained in Chapter 2 were previously published with Joseph Marolla as "Rape and Psychiatric Vocabularies of Motive," in *Gender and Disordered Behavior: Sex Differences in Psychopathology* (E. Gomberg and V. Franks, eds.; Brunner/Mazel, 1979) and as "Rape and Psychiatric Vocabularies of Motive: Alternative Perspectives," in *Rape and Sexual Assault: A Research Handbook* (Ann Wolbert Burgess, ed.; Garland, 1985). Some of the data presented in Chapter 3 were originally published with Joseph Marolla as "Attitudes Toward Women, Violence, and Rape: A Comparison of Convicted Rapists and Other Felons" (*Deviant Behavior*, vol. 7, 1986); parts of Chapters 4 and 5 are a revised and expanded version of an article first published as "Convicted Rapists' Perceptions of Self and Victim: Role-Taking and Emotions" (*Gender and Society*, vol. 2, 1988) and, with Joseph Marolla, "Convicted Rapists' Vocabulary of Motive: Excuses and Justifications" (*Social Problems*, vol. 31, 1984); and part of Chapter 6 is a revised and expanded version of an article with Joseph Marolla first published as "'Riding the Bull at Gilley's': Convicted Rapists Describe the Rewards of Rape" (*Social Problems*, vol. 32, 1985).

1

A Glimpse Inside

This book, which is about men's sexual violence toward women, is the result of several demanding, often frustrating, sometimes gruesome, but always fascinating years in which my research associate, Joseph Marolla, and I entered men's maximum- and medium-security prisons and interviewed 114 convicted rapists as well as a contrast group of 75 other felons. Since research began on these men, I have had the opportunity to present the work to a wide variety of groups—students, academicians, feminists, rape survivors, professionals of all persuasions, the media, and the general public. Audiences always ask two questions: what motivated me to undertake the project, and what kind of an experience was it for me, a woman, to be confined daily in prisons talking face to face with men convicted of rape, murder, and assorted other crimes against women. Curiosity about why and how the research was done is often greater than interest in the findings. Therefore, it seems fitting to begin by reflecting on these questions. And because research inside of prisons, on people confined against their will, is complicated by practical obstacles, ethical dilemmas, and methodological problems that do not customarily occur in investigations of most other groups, it is appropriate to highlight a few of the more perplexing problems that surfaced during the course of this project.

Androcentric Bias in the Sciences

By the late 1960s, higher education in the United States was feeling the impact of the second wave of feminism and the

1

burgeoning women's liberation movement. With the gradual increase of women faculty in college and universities (albeit at lower salaries than men) came an increasing awareness of the extent to which knowledge about women and women's concerns, or women-centered knowledge, was absent from the content of most courses in the traditional disciplines. In response to these omissions, innovative courses, focused on women's experiences and perspectives, were developed that eventually led to the creation of a new academic field—interdisciplinary women's studies. Undoubtedly the effort to establish women's studies in higher education was motivated, in part, by the alienation the founding mothers felt as practitioners committed to bodies of knowledge that ignored or erased the significance of women's experiences, contributions, and problems.

From modest beginnings, new scholarship on women now flourishes in the arts, humanities, natural sciences, and social sciences, and, while the transformation has been more successful in some disciplines than in others,[1] the impact of feminist scholarship is observed not only in college curricula, but in knowledge generally. At the heart of feminist critique in the social sciences are several basic assumptions.[2] We understand that women and men live in separate phenomenological, if not physical, worlds, which means there are important gender differences in our social construction of reality. Because our experiences in and of the world are not the same, the relevances of our worlds are also different.[3] The greater power of men, relative to women, has resulted in knowledge or science that is based primarily on the relevances of a privileged, white, male social universe, supported ideologically by the assumption that the masculine is the yardstick against which all else is compared and judged.[4] Therefore, much of conventional knowledge reflects the tenets of patriarchal ideology despite its claim to be objective science. Feminists argue that these "universal" male truths are irrelevant to women at best, and alienating and oppressive at worst. To correct omissions and distortions of the past, the emphasis, especially in early feminist scholarship, has been on understanding women's world, not by tossing gender in as a variable, but by putting women at the center of research that is nonalienating, nonexploitive, and potentially emancipating. The challenge of feminist scholarship extends beyond filling in the gaps in knowledge about women to shifting or, if necessary, constructing new paradigms that account for women's experiences and perspectives and that contribute to a more complete gendered understanding of the world.

The Need for Feminist Research on Men's World

The significance of this new, intellectually inspiring scholarship on women's world cannot be overstated. Yet I continue to be concerned that feminist scholars are neglecting another, also important, area of critical work on men's world.[5] There are important reasons for concern. If, as evidence suggests, men dominate through an ideology that erases or ignores the significance of women and allows men to take for granted that their social constructions *are* reality, then transforming knowledge, and ultimately patriarchy, requires a challenge of that reality—even though it requires intruding where women are not always welcome. Indeed, the idea of a ruling ideology suggests that men's privileged status distorts their perceptions and understanding of the world. While not diminishing the continuing responsibility to illuminate women's subordinate condition, the debunking of patriarchy is not accomplished by focusing exclusively on the lives and experiences of women.

As an activist in the women's movement of the 1970s, I was impressed by the mounting feminist anger over the sexual victimization of women. To dispel harmful stereotypes and provide a structure for assisting the survivors,[6] it was critical that the experience and trauma of women who had been raped be examined, and, in the late 1970s, feminist scholars enthusiastically tackled this challenge. The new awareness was inspiring vital research on rape myths and the psychological, medical, and legal problems experienced by the victims of rape (see, for example, Burgess and Holmstrom 1974; Holmstrom and Burgess 1978b). This period also witnessed the publication of several groundbreaking theoretical feminist treatises on rape,[7] and sexual violence moved to the center of emerging radical feminist theory on patriarchy and the origins and maintenance of women's subordination. Yet, despite the growing feminist presence in the rape literature, the need for research on sexually violent men was being ignored. Consequently, this area of rape research continued to be dominated by men and the profession of psychiatry. I was concerned that the feminist tendency to focus on women's experience of rape did not go far enough to challenge the prevailing assumption that sexual violence is the result of an individual, idiosyncratic disease (for a full discussion of this point, see Chapter 2), an explanation that my sociological background led me to doubt. Focusing on victimized women also did not constitute enough of a threat to the sexually violent male world in which we live because women are not the clue to men's sexual violence. In fact, focusing on women can lead to blaming the victim and to perceiving rape as women's, rather than men's, problem. Women cannot reveal the motivations and justifications of the men who rape them because they don't share the reality of sexually violent men. Such insight is acquired only through invading and critically examining the social constructions of men who rape.

This concern, as well as my training as a sociologist and my personal experiences as a woman, provided the motivation to do research on sexually violent men—to gain an understanding of how the meanings and relevances of their world differ from mine. Indeed, the gender imbalance of power allows men to ignore women's world, but the subordinate status of women forces us to pay attention to men's world. Rapists are not the only perpetrators of violent and degrading acts toward women, but because of their position at the endpoint of the continuum, they are ideal informants on our sexually violent culture. And that is the purpose of this book: to understand sexual violence from the perspective of men who rape—to provide outsiders with a view inside.

In 1975, Public Law 94-63 established the National Center for the Prevention and Control of Rape in the United States within the National Institute of Mental Health. The Center was mandated to provide funding for research, training, and public education activities in the areas of rape and sexual assault of children and adults.[8] This event was important for women because it signified official recognition of the seriousness of rape and also established a funding source for rape-related research. In 1979, I applied to the National Institute of Mental Health for funds to conduct face-to-face interviews inside of men's prisons because I believed (and still do) that penetrating the male world of sexual violence requires direct, experiential contact with the experts, men who rape. Statistical studies using data from surveys and official sources could not duplicate the range of information and depth of understanding that could be obtained by observing and talking confidentially with the men. The National Institute of Mental Health eventually did support this research, which consisted of 89 pages of semistructured interviews with 114 convicted rapists and a contrast group of 75 other felons—a total of approximately 700 hours of interviews and 15,000 pages of data. Before funding was approved, a number of thorny problems had to be resolved. Important among these was the specific question of whether men convicted of crimes against women would talk about it to a woman and, conversely, whether a woman would be able to talk about rape with them. Other issues concerned general rapport and cooperation, human subject protection, and the validity of truthfulness of the information gathered in the interviews. Before approaching these topics, however, it is necessary to explain the reasons for choosing convicted incarcerated rapists for this research and the limitations imposed by this choice.

Are Convicted Rapists the Best Targets?

Research on rapists is hampered by obstacles in accurately determining the size and characteristics of the male population that rapes as well as by unavoidable restrictions on obtaining a representative sample of sexually violent men. There are several reasons for these problems. First, rape is among the most underreported of major crimes. Most studies estimate that only between 25 percent to 50 percent of completed and attempted rapes are brought to the attention of police (Federal Bureau of Investigation, 1972; Law Enforcement Assistance Administration 1974). Thus, it is certain that a significant proportion of men who rape never enter the criminal justice system at any level and consequently the characteristics of this undetected group cannot be stated with certainty. Victimization research provides insight on some of the factors that affect women's willingness to report rape. In one study of 246 victims who contacted the women-run Seattle Rape Relief, 100 had not reported their rapes to the police (Williams 1984). Analysis revealed that women were more likely to report if the characteristics of their attack resembled a "classic" rape—a sudden, violent attack by a stranger in a public place or a home that was broken into, involving the use of a weapon and resulting in injuries in addition to rape. For a combination of reasons—fear of retaliation from the rapist, fear of not being believed or the stigma of a trial, self-blame, or the desire to protect friends and families—reported rape underrepresents assaults between people who are acquaintances, friends, or relatives; that occur in social situations such as dates; and where verbal threats, rather than more direct forms of violence, are used to make the victim comply.

Additionally, for a number of social and legal reasons, conviction rates for rape have been low relative to other major crimes. For example, in 1978, of the 635 rape complaints that were reported to police in Seattle and Kansas City, criminal cases were prepared on only 167 suspects. Of this number, only 45 cases brought rape or attempted rape charges by prosecutors, 32 cases went to trial, and only 10 defendants—less than 2 percent—were convicted of rape or attempted rape (Law Enforcement Assistance Administration 1978). While convictions may have increased during the past ten years, low rates were the norm when the men in this study were processed by the criminal justice system. In addition to the class and race differences in conviction and sentencing that are a general characteristic of the criminal justice system, because of factors such as biased attitudes regarding what constitutes "real" rape, state statutes that required proof of victim resistance for conviction, and court-room tactics aimed at discrediting the victim, accused rapists who used overt violence and/or weapons and who committed accompanying crimes were more likely to be sent to prison than accused men who did not fit this profile. Rapists in prison, then, are more likely to have raped strangers, used weapons, physically injured their victims, and committed other crimes in addition to the rape. They also are likely to be poorly educated, lacking economic resources, and members of racial minorities.

An ideal research design would include interviews with a proportion of men from the potentially large group of undetected rapists who may not fit the rapist-in-prison profile. In attempts to investigate this population, several researchers have used anonymous questionnaires to identify and measure the characteristics and attitudes of sexually aggressive college men. While not diminishing the significance of knowledge gained through this approach, these efforts are considerably removed from lengthy interviews with undetected rapists about their criminal activity. Even if a large group of these rapists could be located, the dangers and ethical dilemmas involved in such research would be enormous. In the final analysis the researcher would become an accomplice by protecting the identity of men actively engaged in rape. The only realistic alternative is to study convicted incarcerated rapists and to be aware of the ways in which research findings may be skewed due to differences between this group and men who rape but avoid detection and/or prison.

In another sense, however, convicted rapists may be the best group with which to explore the ideas presented in this book. Unlike the psychiatric model, which assumes that pathology or disease causes rape, the feminist/sociocultural model pursued herein locates the predisposition for sexual violence in the gender imbalance of power in patriarchal societies (for a complete discussion of this model, see Chapter 2). Of all men who rape, those in prison are most likely to fit the psychiatric model and the least likely to fit the feminist/sociocultural model, making them an ideal test of these conflicting explanations.

7

At the time this research was conducted, no national profile of convicted or incarcerated rapists existed.[9] Thus, while ideally the typicalness of a sample should be established, it was not possible to determine whether the rapists incarcerated in the southeastern state where this research was done were similar to prison populations of rapists nationwide. Other researchers have noted the same problem and have concluded only that rapists who become available for study from prison populations tend to be poorly educated and from low-status occupations (Dietz 1978).

A detailed description of the characteristics of the 114 convicted rapists and 75 other felons interviewed in this research is contained in Chapter 3. Briefly, as expected, the rapists were poorly educated and held low-status jobs prior to going to prison. Most were serving sentences for more than one crime, including 11 percent who had convictions for first- or second-degree murder, and the sentences ranged from 10 years to 7 life sentences plus 380 years. Of the rapists in this sample, 46 percent were white and 54 percent were black; the majority were young, less than 35 years old when interviewed.

All of the participants were volunteers who were recruited by letters sent to every inmate in the seven prisons used in the project. Obviously, a random selection of the men would have been preferable, but ethical limitations typically force research of this nature to rely on volunteers. Often, however, volunteers have characteristics that are different from those of the average member of the group they are used to represent. For example, compared to a statistical profile of all felons in this state, it appears that men who volunteered were disproportionately white, somewhat better educated (at the time of the research), and slightly younger than the average inmate. On the positive side, using volunteers avoided a major methodological problem present in much of the research on convicted rapists that has been conducted by prison staff, such as psychologists and psychiatrists. Since therapists tend to use their own clients as research subjects (for example, see Groth 1979), only men who have sought counseling and who believe their behavior was caused by an emotional or psychological problem are included in these studies. In contrast, volunteers from the prison system at large included a large number of men who neither defined themselves as rapists nor thought of themselves as emotionally disturbed. This book will demonstrate the importance of this distinction.

Lasting Impressions:
A Woman's View of Life Inside Men's Prisons

For most readers unfamiliar with the environment inside of prisons, words are inadequate to describe the shock one experiences as the gates slam shut. Men's prisons are bleak, severe, depressing places, swarming with people and at the same time barren.[10] While common stereotypes of male prisoners may be too extreme, and conditions inside institutions vary, prison culture seems to breed bored, frightened, angry, and very lonely men who believe that survival depends on constant vigilance and a tough facade. Externally, at least, traditional male role behavior is exaggerated. Manhood is validated through physical strength and aggression. Expressions like anger are expected and acceptable but emotional sensitivity to others or the appearance of caring is regarded as dangerous.[11] Any display of characteristics or behavior traditionally associated with the feminine is scorned and avoided. Confined men do not trust other people, including other inmates, and they don't talk to each other about matters of personal or emotional importance. In prison, any display of emotional sensitivity is interpreted as weakness, and, because weakness means vulnerability, the men keep their feelings private. Kept to oneself, personal information can't be used detrimentally when it is in someone's interest to do so. Friendship, in the sense of a trusted person to confide in, does not seem to exist in men's prisons, not even, I discovered, among brothers. While a lack of emotional intimacy may characterize male relations generally, unlike men outside, many of the men inside also lack female confidantes. Indeed, men's prisons are very lonely, desperate places.

I became acutely aware of this peculiar (to me) environment the first day in prison when I realized that, although an unfamiliar woman is hardly a common sight in the yard, no one was looking at me. To be more precise, no one made eye contact with me or with anyone else. It quickly became apparent that walking in the yard requires learning not to look or appear to see, lest a casual glance be interpreted as provocation, a challenge, or a threat. I learned to assume a public posture like that of the men—head cast at a downward angle, peripheral vision intact. In particular, I was very careful never to indicate that I recognized any of the men that I had interviewed because it would have been interpreted as a betrayal of their trust and confidence. Likewise, the men I knew never acknowledged me in the yard. For example, during his interview one young man explained that if he saw me in the yard and other men were present, he would have to act smart and make wisecracks. He wanted me to know he didn't mean it. Friendliness is definitely not a prominent feature of any men's prison I have been in.

Prison yards are cold and indifferent places, but I never really felt fearful even on the rare occasions when Joe and I walked alone, without the protection of a guard. At the same time, I wasn't naive either and I was always aware of the potential for danger. But like the men confined there, I adjusted, and gradually, over months of daily experience, felt more comfortable. Indeed, a year and seven prisons later, one day at a medium-security facility where it was permitted, Joe and I chose to eat with the men in the prisoners' mess rather than in the staff dining hall. Such an act would have been unthinkable that first day.

Not surprisingly, prison officials weren't trusted by the men, but neither were counselors and therapists. Thus, the staff whose purpose it was to attend to the social and emotional needs of the inmates were viewed with suspicion and used primarily for posting gripes and making requests. A true counselor-client relationship is compromised inside prison because therapists are agents of the state, not professionals with loyalties to their clients as on the outside, and the privilege of confidentiality is, at best, weakened. The men believed that information given in a therapy session might be used against them in a parole hearing. Since everyone's principal goal is to get out, the tendency is for the men to tell

10

counselors and therapists what they think the counselors want to hear. Often, during an interview, someone would volunteer a piece of information, indicating it was something he would not tell his counselor. Because of this situation, the validity of much staff-conducted prison research is questionable.

Would the lack of trust and suspicious nature of prison life actually work to the advantage of this research? Incarcerated men, of course, do have feelings. Since they could not, or would not, confide in anyone inside, we hoped that some of the men would welcome the opportunity to discuss issues of personal concern with someone outside of the prison system if for no other reason than to break the tedium of prison routine—provided they were protected by the promise of confidentiality. But would they talk to a woman?

In the Company of Rapists

The fact that I was a woman was a major concern among some reviewers at the National Institute of Mental Health, who questioned how men convicted of rape would respond to a woman. In addition to the issue of safety, they wondered (and so did I) what kind of response a woman would evoke when interviewing rapists on intimate and sensitive details about their crimes. Simply, would rapists talk to a woman, or would they prefer the camaraderie offered by a man?

Indeed, the effect of gender on interviewing is an important methodological question, but at the time of this research, little had been written on the subject. Perhaps this is because the world of research has been monopolized by men, who, reflective of their dominant status, never considered the possibility that their gender (and their politics) might be affecting their data. It is precisely such blindness that raises questions about the assumed impenetrability of the scientific method to bias—an observation that is at the heart of the feminist critique of science. (See, for example, Bleier 1984; Harding 1986; Harding and O'Barr 1987; also see the following special journal issues on feminism and science: *Hypatia*, Vol. 2, fall 1987, and Vol. 3, spring 1988; and *Women's Studies International Forum*, spring 1989.) The scant literature that did address the gender issue suggested that the content of the interview is important. When the topic is neutral, it makes little difference whether the interviewer is male or female. However, when sexual interpretations are involved, male interviewers obtain fewer responses than female interviewers, particularly when the subjects are men. Similarly, research on client–counselor relationships indicates that male counselors elicit more information-seeking responses in contrast to female counselors, who provoke greater self-disclosure and emotional expressivity (for a review of the literature, see Rumenik et al. 1977). This is consistent with other evidence suggesting that while men find it difficult to express their feelings to anyone, they are more likely to confide in women (particularly in women with whom they are involved sexually) because the traditional male gender role proscribes emotional intimacy among men.

Based on the limited methodological literature and because men in prison are particularly inclined toward exhibiting traditional masculinity, there was some reason to predict that rapists might actually talk more openly to a female interviewer. Experience with this project seems to support this speculation. Although Joe and I were both able to establish rapport and obtain information, it appears that more personal information was volunteered to me and, also, my interviews lasted longer. Additionally, a few of the men agreed to be interviewed only if they could be interviewed by a woman. Ironically, even though the topic was crime against women, these men seemed to find it easier and more natural to talk to a woman.[12]

The men were also curious about me. Some of them found it difficult to apprehend the motives of a woman who would voluntarily get involved in prison research. They wanted to know about my personal life, particularly whether I was married. I discovered that men in prison are always looking for a "girl" friend and, thus, I found it expedient to resume wearing a discarded wedding ring since the property of another man is "off limits," more or less. They were also curious about my relationship with Joe. The concept of a professional relationship between people of opposite sexes was simply foreign to many of the men, who believed that sex is always, or should be, part of such arrangements.

The idea of being cloistered alone and unprotected for hours with a man convicted of rape and assorted other violent crimes is intimidating to almost everyone, including me. Especially early in the project, I felt a generalized sense of anxiousness that was intensified by some anonymous telephone calls and several threatening letters that I had received. For security purposes, I took the precaution of removing my home address from all public records, such as at the university and local telephone company and having my phone number unlisted. In the final analysis, however, I had to admit and accept the potential for risk. As I became more accustomed to prison, the desire to get good data became the driving force, and I learned to put the professional self before the personal self.

It was not a typical experience, but there were a few interviews in which I felt concerned about safety. For confidentiality purposes, all interviews were conducted in private, out of earshot of the guard posted in the vicinity. Probably the most threatening experience was with a young man, convicted of rape and murder, who believed that rape was a man's right. Women, he insisted, must always submit. During the course of his interview, he became visibly angrier and angrier at my probing until finally he leaned across the table and offered me a simple choice—would I prefer that he rape me or murder me? I suggested that there were other alternatives, and reminded him that I was not the subject of the interview. I must admit to being especially relieved when his interview was over.

The Interview: A Social Encounter

Adding to the difficulty of the research, it had been agreed that in order to minimize disruption in the cooperating institutions, one long interview, rather than several short ones, would be conducted with each of the participants. And the interviews were long—for rapists, 89 pages divided into three parts: Part 1 consisting of a complete background history including childhood, family, religious, marital, education, employment, sexual, and criminal; Part 2 consisting of a series of scales measuring attitudes toward women, masculinity, interpersonal violence, and rape; and Part 3 consisting of 40 pages of open-ended questions about the rape and the victim. Those in the contrast group of other felons were given only Part 1 and 2 of the interview. This raised the issue of whether one session, regardless of interviewer gender, was sufficient to develop the amount of rapport and trust needed to obtain information of a highly sensitive nature.

Indeed, the success of this research hinged on the ability to develop a good working relationship within a very brief span of time. The interviews were fragile, easily destroyed by a careless remark or gesture; they were hard work and they were stressful, draining experiences for all of us—researchers and men alike. During the first hour, men who by habit were untrusting and suspicious had to be placed at ease and made to feel it was safe to divulge personal information that under usual conditions they would be unwilling to discuss at all.

Because the focus of the research was on threatening and illegal behavior, subjects that most people would find difficult to discuss even under the best of conditions, the format of the interview and the ordering of topics was of critical importance. Conventional wisdom aside, research has found that it makes little difference whether threatening questions are asked face-to-face, over the telephone, or in self-administered questionnaires. The ways in which questions are asked, however, do make a difference. Essentially, the reporting of stigmatized behavior can be increased through the use of long introductions to threatening topics and open-ended questions (Bradburn and Sudman 1979). So, for example, before asking a man about his sexual history, an area of potential embarrassment, I gave him a brief introduction to the topic and essentially gave him permission to express himself honestly. Many of the men were genuinely uncomfortable with these intrusive questions, but, because they were presented this way, almost all were willing to discuss even the most intimidating of subjects.

Despite methodological convention, I also found that it was impossible to adhere to a rigid sequence for questions. Quite simply, no matter how much probing was done, the men would not talk about certain things until they were ready and felt comfortable. So although all of the questions were asked of every man, the interviews, rather than being uniform, were all slightly different, depending on the needs and readiness of the interviewee. Further, the social distance between us was minimized by assuming an air of conversation rather than a more formal interview style. The length of the interview, 89 pages, also helped to lessen the impact of personal and threatening topics. Because so much background information of a neutral, nonthreatening nature was gathered early in the interview, it was possible to build gradually to the more sensitive areas of sexual and criminal history and details about the rape(s). Without this gradual, flexible, cumulative approach, interspersed with friendly chatter, it is highly doubtful that some of the data presented in this book could have been obtained.

The critical importance of sound initial groundwork became painfully clear during an interview one day when, just as I began the sexual history, a power outage left us in complete darkness in our windowless room. The men were rounded up and hustled into lockup. The next day, assuming sufficient rapport had been established the previous day, I tried to resume the interview where we had left off. The obviously very embarrassed young man abruptly asked to be excused for a minute, and I never saw him again (although I trust the prison staff did). This was a hard lesson, because interviews were often complicated to arrange and every one of them was of immense value to the project. I had foolishly broken a cardinal rule, and I took care never to repeat that mistake.

Physical cues, such as changes in face work and body language, were the best signals that conditions were suitable for proceeding with the more sensitive parts of the interview. For example, one of my most difficult interviews was with a member of one of the more notorious motorcycle gangs, who was in prison for abduction and rape. As soon as he entered the room, I knew I was in for a difficult time. He was covered with tattoos, suggestive of his involvement in gang activities, and swastikas, symbolizing his less-than-admirable political views; his head was wrapped in a bandanna, and,

15

most important, he wore mirror-front sunglasses, making eye contact impossible. In other words, he had come to the interview fully cloaked in protective armor. Further, he positioned himself in the chair so that he faced the wall, not me. I had only a side view of his face. In every way he dripped contempt, making his dislike for me as well as all other "straights" perfectly clear. Gradually, and with great hesitation, he began to answer questions in monosyllables and I kept wondering why he had volunteered for research he so clearly disdained. After some 45 minutes I decided drastic action was necessary. Since it was clear he wasn't going to talk, it was worth risking the interview. Abruptly, I asked him why he had volunteered for the research since he clearly neither liked what I represented nor planned to talk to me. "Because I'm curious," he grudgingly conceded. But the question seemed to catch him off guard and signaled a turning point in the interview. First the head gear came off, then the mirror glasses, so that I could make eye contact with him. His body shifted to face me, even leaning inward. At this point I knew it was safe to proceed with more sensitive topics. By the end of the interview he appeared completely relaxed, and, feet up on the table between us, he refused to end the interview, asked permission to be excused from lunch, and attempted to persuade me to go out with one of his "brothers" on the outside. As it turned out, this was one of the most informative interviews I did.

In the final analysis and despite the problems, I discovered, as initially suspected, that even the most hardened felon would talk, with varying degrees of openness, to an interested, supportive, nonjudgmental outsider if for no other reason than to break the tedium of prison routine. Beyond a doubt, the key to establishing rapport was to create, from the very beginning, a sense of mutual respect and trust, and absolute confidentiality. The staff—inmate split and routinized rule-bound existence in prisons typically results in dehumanized treatment of inmates, who, as the inferiors, are handled with rigid authoritarianism. It facilitated rapport to let the men know that from a research perspective, they were the experts and the researcher's job was to record what they had to say. Then, too, some of the men volunteered because they were desperately in need of a confidant or confessor, someone who would allow them to ventilate their feelings. Even though the research nature of the interview was explained, a number of the men described their experience as therapeutic or cathartic (although not in those words) and, while it may tax the imagination, a few even cried.

Thus, I found that it was possible for excessive rapport to develop. Excessive rapport made terminating some of the interviews difficult—an unexpected situation since the prime concern had been establishing rapport—and it required the same amount of delicacy as initial groundwork. A typical experience was to conclude the interview with a thank you while the man remained firmly rooted in his chair and continued to talk, asking to be kept out of count or to miss a meal. In this extended fashion the time allocated for a session was frequently surpassed, and some of my interviews exceeded five hours; there was one memorable session in solitary confinement with a man who had raped and murdered five women in which we talked for seven hours without a break.

From the perspective of the men, once a sense of trust had been established, there was a tendency to want to preserve the relationship. It was also clear that after their self-disclosures, many of the men wanted and expected some feedback. Essentially they were asking me to abandon my nonjudgmental, neutral role and tell them what I thought of them, their crimes, and, in some cases, whether they were likely to rape again. A mystique had developed in which I was being credited with much more wisdom and insight than I possessed. These situations were handled by letting the man know that his cooperation had been especially helpful and appreciated, that while his criminal acts were deplorable, he also had good qualities and was capable of constructive behavior. I wanted everyone to be able to exit the interview, although possibly drained, feeling good about his participation.

Several of the men attempted to maintain contact by writing to me in the months following their interviews. Their letters were often sensitive and moving. For example, this was written from the hospital by a rapist serving seven life sentences:

The other morning as I layed here in bed I could here the birds across the street in the tree's singing. Tears sprang to my eyes as I realized how long it had been since this beautiful sound had entertained me in the morning. I thought of how wonderful it would be to simply lay on the grass under a tree and gaze at the sky & clouds. All of this, I'm sure sounds silly. But faced with what I have to deal with, I believe I'd be very willing to give my life up just to do these simple, but delightful things, if for only a few hours. . . . I don't know what the answer is—but I know that prison is only a place where bitterness, hate, loneliness and fantasy lives and breeds.

Over time, they stopped writing.

Rapport is an interactive process, so, as unlikely as it may seem, I found that it was also possible for me to develop unexpected empathy occasionally during the course of an interview. This is not an unusual research experience. In fact, it could be argued that the ability to see things from the perspective of the other is a necessary precondition for acquiring an insider's subjective understanding of the other's reality. I had had the same experience while conducting my previous research on residents in obstetrics and gynecology. In both cases, objectivity returned rapidly when the field experience was over. Such emotions may be more expected when the subjects are people with a sympathetic cause. Yet convicted rapists too are human.

One final aspect of rapport and researcher neutrality deserves mention. The type of information sought in this research required a supportive, nonjudgmental, neutral facade—one that I did not always genuinely feel. Frankly, some of the men were personally repulsive, such as the one who positioned a "spit bucket" on the table between us and periodically sent missiles of dripping chewing tobacco hurling in my direction. I left that interview too nauseated to eat lunch. Additionally, the stories they told were horrible, and a few of the men were not overly cooperative. Indeed, some of the interviews required immense effort to remain neutral. But the fact is that no one tells his or her secrets to a visibly hostile and disapproving person. There were times, however, when I felt my effort to secure data through nonjudgmental means was being misunderstood and might have unintended consequences. This was especially problematic with the men (referred to in this book as *deniers*) who did not define their sexually violent behavior as rape. I worried that some of these men might interpret neutrality as a signal of agreement or approval—certainly not what I wanted to communicate. At the same time, disagreement or negative comments could destroy the rapport so vital to a successful interview. Such responses might also compromise future interviews within that prison. If word got around, and it would, who would volunteer to get shot down by the researcher? I had faced a similar dilemma in my previous research on residency training in obstetrics and gynecology when I witnessed women being talked into unnecessary surgery. In both cases, I did what circumstances permitted without destroying the research environment. If a man requested my opinion of his behavior at the end of the interview, I gave it, candidly but carefully, so that he was able to leave feeling reasonably positive about his participation. This is an important issue in research of this nature, and one of which future investigators should be aware.

Protecting the Rights of Participants

The historical abuse of people used as the objects of biomedical and behavioral research is legendary. Among the more notorious examples are the Tuskegee syphilis experiment in which treatment was deliberately withheld from 400 black men in order to observe the debilitating, often fatal, progression of unchecked syphilis; the diethylstilbestrol (DES) experiments in which pregnant women were told they were taking vitamins rather than DES, which later proved to be carcinogenic in their daughters; and the Stanford prison project in which students were locked in and refused permission to leave a mock prison at Stanford University so that researchers could observe the effects of confinement on behavior. Public attitudes also reflect a callous disregard for human life. For example, a local newspaper carried a recent letter to the editor urging the use of criminals in medical research to save the lives of laboratory animals (*Richmond* [VA] *News Leader* May 11, 1988). For valid reasons, the protection of subjects is no longer left to the discretion of individual researchers. In 1974, the National Research Act was signed into law, creating a national commission that was charged with establishing a structure to oversee research involving human beings. Included in this structure are Institutional Review Boards (consisting of institutional and community representatives) that must approve and monitor all research in institutions, like universities, that receive federal funds. Some researchers have been critical of the federal guidelines, complaining that they have made good research difficult and, in some cases, have amounted to censorship. Ethically, the question is, To what limits is it permissible to use human beings in the name of science?

Research involving certain groups that are particularly vulnerable or at risk, including pregnant women, children, people with impaired judgment such as the mentally retarded, and residents of penal and psychiatric facilities, is monitored with an extra measure of caution. Thus, because this research involved incarcerated men, human subject protection was a paramount concern. Further complicating the situation, procedures for handling voluntary informed consent, risk reduction, and confidentiality had to be agreed upon by three separate bodies, each with slightly different priorities—the University Institutional Review Board, the State Department of Corrections, and the National Institute of Mental Health. Along the way, the project was blocked by legal and ethical dilemmas that transcend any individual undertaking. The final resolution, although not perfect, required over a year of effort that delayed the start of the project. As one example, just before final approval of funding by the National Institute of Mental Health, the NIMH review panel discovered that the University Institutional Review Board had been insufficiently constituted when it approved the research because it lacked a member who represented prisoner interests. After some amount of searching, a former inmate was located, and he generously reviewed, approved, and continued to monitor the project. Because the protection of the human subjects of research is a fundamental, and in this case complicated, issue, some elaboration is appropriate.

Imprisoned people present unique problems related to obtaining voluntary informed consent. In fact, it can be argued that inmate status, combined with the need to appear cooperative to prison officials and parole boards, limits the exercise of judgment and free choice. This concern dictated both the method for recruiting participants and the composition of the control group.

To minimize the potential for coercion in recruiting volunteers, every man in each of the seven host prisons was contacted by letter and told that two professors from a local university were conducting research that involved interviewing men in prison about their attitudes toward sexual behavior and women. If they were willing to participate, they were instructed to complete a brief form requesting name, age, race, education, previous occupation, and current and previous convictions, and to mail it in the provided postage-paid envelope to the university. The letter also explained that it would not be possible to interview everyone who volunteered, prompting a number of men to write long notes detailing why they thought they should be one of the chosen. This procedure allowed a purposeful sample, based on known characteristics, to be constructed. Equally important, nonparticipation could not be held against any individual, since he may have been a volunteer who was not selected to be interviewed.

The contact letter did not mention that rapists were the focus of the research. Within prison hierarchies, sex offenders, particularly child molesters but also certain types of rapists, have low status. Because of this and personal embarrassment and shame, some convicted rapists prefer to conceal the nature of their offense from other inmates. Thus, there was reason to expect that the volunteer rate would be low if participants were solicited from among convicted rapists only. Additionally, unnecessary risk might have accrued to the men who did volunteer, thus branding themselves as rapists within the prison community. Thus, to protect the anonymity of the rapists, it was necessary to interview an almost equal number of men who did not have convictions for rape or other sexual offenses. Since a large number (75) of other felons had to be interviewed anyway, constraints on time and money led to using them as a comparison on background and attitude data. Although a control group of nonfelons would have been preferable, this design avoided an important methodological problem in much of the psychiatrically oriented research, which has focused on differences among categories of sex offenders, for example, between rapists and child molesters. I contend that the most relevant comparison is between rapists and other men whose sexual preference is adult women, and the other felons met this criterion (for an elaboration on this point, see Chapter 3).

The consent procedure was elaborate, involving the use of three separate forms, each signed and witnessed in the presence of a prison representative. In addition to a full explanation of risks and safeguards, each man was advised he could refuse to answer any of the questions, had the right to terminate the interview at any time, and would be given the option of destroying the interview at the conclusion of the session if he so desired. Permission to view prison records, used to check the validity of the interview data, was also obtained.

Although time-consuming, the consent procedure was not a waste of time. It was a serious matter to the men, none of whom opted to destroy his interview. It helped to generate the trust so vital to establishing rapport and emphasized the most critical fact—that we were not connected with the prison or with the Department of Corrections. Without this assurance, much of this book would not exist.

This research did not carry the potential for physical harm, but other risks were present. Most serious was the issue of confidentiality—what information would be protected and how. Because the men were interviewed about past criminal activities, there was the possibility that they could reveal information unknown to the authorities. The reviewers at the National Institute of Mental Health questioned how information of this nature would or should be treated.

Under certain circumstances, I believe that researchers have an obligation to protect their informants even when the information they give is useful to authorities. In the case of past criminal behavior, confidentiality is justified because past acts do not pose a current threat and, since the individual is already in prison, no one is placed in danger from the continued activity. Likewise, the confidentiality of details about ongoing illegal activities that occur within prisons, involving things like drugs or sexual behavior, can be defended. Since staff are generally aware that these activities exist to some degree in all prisons, informing about a specific act would contribute little to what is already known or to a solution. In the case of both types of information, confidentiality is justified in light of the magnitude and seriousness of rape and the fact that good research can be done only if informants can be guaranteed they will not suffer as a consequence of being truthful.

It is necessary, however, to make a distinction between the researcher's obligation to an informant when information concerns past activities and when the information relates to a future act that poses danger to another person. In the latter case, protection of the endangered person takes precedence over the rights of the informant. It is precisely this situation that makes research on undetected felons nearly impossible. In anticipation of the possibility that plans for future acts could be revealed during an interview, all participants were warned of the conditions under which confidential information would be revealed to authorities—if it involved a future act that constituted a serious threat to another's life or well-being, if it was directed at a specific person (not vague or global threats), and if it included a realistic plan of action as well as a reasonable opportunity to carry it out.

Ironically, the major challenge to confidentiality involved a threat against me. Shortly after entering one of the prisons, I began to receive a series of threatening letters from an inmate who identified himself as Count Dracula, as well as by name and number. A check revealed he was a convicted rapist, although not one who had volunteered for the research. In his obscene and repulsive letters, he claimed to have determined that I was to be his mate, and planned to commit what amounted to abduction and rape. The letters were frightening, but because the lack of opportunity precluded a clear danger, I decided against showing them to the warden. I was also aware that reporting him might have interfered with the ability to conduct future interviews in that prison.

Having guaranteed confidentiality, the task remained to devise a plan that assured the promise could be kept. Researchers are placed in an untenable predicament: on the one hand, they are ethically obligated to protect their informants; on the other, they are denied the legal right to do so. Further, the period just prior to this research had witnessed several cases in which search warrants were used to gain access to researchers' files. The data, then, had to be handled in a way that reduced the risk of seizure or subpoena, and this concern also shaped the research endeavor.

One precaution was to sacrifice tape-recording the interviews in favor of recording by hand, because legally, unlike a voiceprint, hand-recorded material is considered hearsay. This compromise both aided and hindered the research. The absence of a tape recorder probably increased the men's willingness to speak candidly. At the same time, hand recording a long interview is exhausting. While the abilities to record conversation verbatim and to think one thing while saying another increase with practice, inevitably some data are lost. Subtlety of tone and nuance of meaning cannot be recorded by hand. Because it is not possible to capture every word on paper, it is constantly necessary to make decisions about what not to record. In this way, important information may be missed because its significance has yet to crystallize. For example, it was not until well into the analysis of the data that the frequency and significance of rapists' remarks about their victims' alleged interest in cunnilingus became apparent. Since, elsewhere in the interview, oral sex was most frequently mentioned by them as a sexual behavior of which most people disapprove, their remarks can be interpreted as another attempt to discredit their victims. (For a full discussion of rapists' justifications, see Chapter 4.)

Concern over the possibility of search and seizure made storing and analyzing the data especially problematic. At the end of each prison day, consent forms, which did contain names, were separated from interviews, which did not contain names, and both were secured as quickly as possible in an anonymous bank safety deposit vault, immune from search warrants. Because the data could not be analyzed from a bank vault, it was necessary to divide each interview into two parts identified by a common identification number, one part containing history, background, and attitude scales, and the other part containing information about crime(s). While one part of the interview was being analyzed at the university, the other remained in the bank vault. This system allowed for greater control over unpredictable events, but hauling 15,000 pages of interviews back and forth also made analyzing the data far more complicated than usual. And paying for the vault required elaborate bureaucratic maneuvering because the auditors who handled grant finances were not permitted to know the name or location of the bank.

Despite these precautions, the reviewers at the National Institute of Mental Health raised the question of what would be done if a court order was used to force disclosure of the data—another example of the web of conflicting rights and responsibilities in which researchers are caught. In the case of this project, I believe it would have been justified to resist a court order because the concealed information would not have endangered another person. As a legal remedy in the case of a subpoena, I secured a Certificate of Confidentiality from the (then) U.S. Department of Health, Education and Welfare. Although at that time the Certificate of Confidentiality had not been tested in court, it theoretically could have been used as a basis for moving to quash a court order. Thus, there was also the possibility that it could fail, leaving only two options: comply and reveal confidential information or be held in contempt of court with the possibility of a fine and/or a prison sentence. Fortunately, none of this happened and my commitment to the principle was not tested. However, the possibility that it could have happened is a sad commentary on the exigencies under which researchers must work. Undoubtedly, it is also a deterrent to research on difficult groups and sensitive topics.

Do Convicts "Con"?

Researchers are generally wary of prisoners because they have the reputation for being more prone to lying, fabrication, and manipulation than other groups. Indeed, several studies appear to confirm this impression. For example, based on physiological measurement of erection response, several studies have found that rapists underreported the extent of their arousal from audiotaped rape depictions (Abel et al. 1977, 1978). In other studies, pedophiles faked their responses to stimuli involving children in order to produce response patterns they thought would appear normal to the therapist (Laws and Holman 1978), and aggressors in prison homosexual activities played down the unwillingness of their partners (Sagarin 1976).

Considering the circumstances of these prison studies and what might be lost by honesty, it is hardly surprising that the men attempted to respond in a manner they thought would gain them approval. Indeed, research on all groups is compromised to some extent by the cultural tendency to give socially desirable responses. But, in addition, the client-subject role carries an implicit threat because parole or release can depend on the assessment of the therapist-researcher. We attempted to lessen the effect of social desirability by stressing confidentiality and the fact that nothing said in an interview would have any impact, positive or negative, on prison or parole status.

Although the purpose of the research was to obtain the men's own perceptions of their acts, it was also necessary to establish the extent to which these perceptions deviated from other descriptions of their crimes. Therefore, after each interview, with the permission of the man, we checked records to establish the validity of the interview information.[13] A list of 30 questions was developed related to general background and details of the crime—the type of factual information usually found in presentence reports[14] on file at prisons. There was a disadvantage to embarking on an interview without any prior knowledge. Obviously, misinformation could not be challenged unless it was obvious or illogical enough that it naturally aroused suspicion.

Based on their versions of their crimes and the information contained in their records, three distinct types of rapists emerged. The largest group consisted of 47 men who are labeled *admitters* because they admitted to raping their victims and there were no substantial discrepancies between information they gave in the interviews and the facts contained in their records. Nonetheless, while admitters did not attempt to alter the facts, they did systematically understate the amount of force and violence they used, which was often more than needed to accomplish the rape. To get this kind of detail, persistent, forceful probing was necessary. Admitters also did not volunteer information about especially brutal or offensive aspects of their crimes. For example, a particularly anguished young man tearfully recounted the details of his rape, including the age of his 70-year-old victim. His self-disgust was further clarified when the validity check revealed what he neglected to mention—that the victim had been his grandmother and that she suffered a heart attack as a result of the rape. Such omissions did not alter expressions of guilt, but they were the types of details that were impossible to reveal to another person and, at the same time, save face. Thus, even the most cooperative men also attempted to mute their negative image—a response I consider normal.

A second group of 33 rapists are labeled *deniers*, and in many ways they are more interesting than admitters. These men acknowledged having had sexual contact with their victims but did not admit that their actions constituted rape. The details they gave in the interviews were similar to their versions of the crime contained in the records, but they were obviously different from the victims' versions. A few deniers were in transition and, more than likely, eventually would admit to their crimes, in the same way that a few admitters confided that at one time they had denied. However, the majority seemed genuinely to believe their actions were not rape despite the admission, in some cases, that a weapon had been used.

There are a number of ways that denials have been interpreted. They have been dismissed as lies; they have been translated as evidence of ego protection—a way to avoid admitting to oneself one's capacity for committing detestable acts; and they have been seen as an expression of social desirability and an attempt to negotiate a nondeviant identity with others. But denials can also be taken at face value, and the content analyzed as a statement on the cultural learning and socially derived perspective of sexually violent men. I hope to demonstrate that a major key to understanding sexual violence as a social phenomenon rests with what rapists have to tell us about how men in this society have learned to justify and excuse their violent degradation of women. The content of denials forms a major part of this understanding.

The third group of 34 men denied outright any sexual contact with their victims. Instead, they said that they themselves were the victims of mistaken identity, or that they had not raped the victims but had committed other crimes against them, such as robbery, or that they had been in the victims' presence while someone else raped them. Because these men claimed to have no knowledge of the rapes they were convicted of, they are omitted from the discussion in Chapters 4, 5, and 6, but they are included in the analysis of background and attitude data in Chapter 3.[15]

Trials and Tribulations of Prison Research

One final note on prison research. Overall, the men who participated in this project were more cooperative and polite than I had anticipated. At times I was made to feel as a guest in their home—as indeed I was. For example, in a small experimental program within a large maximum-security prison, where the men lived cottage style without some of the restrictions that apply within the larger setting, I was shown around the facility with pride by one of the men I interviewed. He also supplied me with soft drinks, and cookies that he had baked for the occasion.

Likewise, the cooperation of the State Department of Corrections and the staffs of the seven prisons used in this research was beyond my expectation. Before entering each prison, an official from the Department of Corrections accompanied us to an initial meeting with the warden, where the research was explained and the procedures for recruiting volunteers and scheduling and conducting interviews were elaborated. Due to these generous efforts, two of us were able to complete 189 interviews in a little over a year.

Still, prisons are special places, and there are obstacles in this kind of research that are not encountered when the target of inquiry is a noninstitutionalized population. The interviewing process went smoothly most of the time, but, inevitably, due to the nature of prisons there were also frustrating delays and extenuating circumstances that could be neither anticipated nor controlled. For example, in one prison a riot and subsequent lockup delayed the project for over a month. This prison continued to experience unrest during the three months we spent there, which increased the already considerable suspiciousness of the inmates. In fact, several men volunteered to be interviewed with the hope of persuading us to intercede on behalf of the lawsuits they wanted to bring against the prison or to contact lawyers for them. When they discovered that we would not interfere in prison politics, they were unhappy—to put it mildly.

Prisons were entered one at a time, and all interviews at one were completed as quickly as possible before we moved to the next location. It was a hectic schedule, but the longer we spent in an institution, the more rumors tended to spread about the research. To minimize the influence of gossip on the data, we attempted to expedite the interview process, but this was not always possible. Maddening delays occurred due to scheduling mishaps, inmate transfers, and occasional no-shows. In one prison, we were often turned away at the gate because someone had neglected to inform the guard we were coming—even though we were there every day for three months. In another prison, a series of power outages cut the workday short and necessitated the rescheduling of interviews. A drug bust in another prison complicated the procedure for searching us as we entered and exited.

The adequacy of interview facilities was uniformly poor. Locating two private empty rooms was almost always a problem, and sometimes meant dislocating someone else. As a result, interviews were held anywhere that met the basic requirement of privacy and soundproofing, including classrooms, libraries, chapels, barbershops, isolation cells, and trailers. I recall two particularly memorable days, one spent interviewing while sitting on beds in the dispensary examining room, and another spent in a telephone booth! The prison requirement that a guard be stationed in the vicinity of the interviewing drained already limited resources and did little to increase our popularity among the staff. Beyond a doubt, however, the roughest times were the two summers spent in the prisons. Typical of southern climate, it was blistering hot and humid as a swamp, but most of the time interviews were done without the benefit of air conditioning. By the end of a day, the usually small room would be unbearable, as, dripping with sweat, we attempted to concentrate through the ripple of heat waves between us. The men who suffered through these interviews deserve a special thanks. In short, anyone contemplating research in a prison setting is best advised to be patient and to expect anything.

Notes

1 For a discussion of the natural and physical sciences, see Harding (1986). For a discussion of the humanities and social sciences, see Stacey and Thorne (1985).
2 For a general discussion of this issue, see Hooks (1981), Hull et al. (1982), Sherma and Beck (1979), Smith (1974), and Bach Zinn (1982).
3 For a full discussion of gender differences in the social construction of reality, see Smith (1979).
4 For example, Carol Gilligan (1982) critiques Piaget and Kohlberg for excluding girls from their research on the stages of moral development. Her revision of Piaget and Kohlberg has itself sparked a conceptual and methodological debate among feminist scholars. See Kerber et al. (1986).
5 Most of the critical work on men and masculinity has been done by men. For example, see Brod (1986) and Pleck (1981).
6 Throughout this book I refer to women who have been raped as *victims*, mindful that *survivors* is the currently preferred term. Within the context of what I am discussing, *victims* seems a more appropriate choice. Then, too, not all women survive.
7 Prominent among these were Brownmiller (1975), Griffin (1971), Medea and Thompson (1974), and Russell (1975).
8 For a history of NCPCR, see Lystad (1985).

9   In an effort to develop a profile of rapists, I contacted a random selection of states and requested demographic data on their incarcerated rapists. I was surprised to discover that, at the time of this research, most states did not accumulate such data.

10 I have never been inside any women's prisons and thus cannot compare them to men's facilities.

11 For a discussion of the traditional male gender role, see Pleck (1981).

12 In retrospect, race was also a consideration in this research. It is unfortunate, but true, that prisons intensify the racial tensions in society generally. The lack of interaction between black men and white men is noticeable. The degree to which the life experiences of black men in a racist world and daily life in a tense environment affected their ability to be candid with white interviewers cannot be calculated. It did not prevent black men from volunteering or from cooperating with us, nor was it overly difficult to establish rapport with the 54 percent of participants who were black. Nonetheless, I believe these men would have been more comfortable and candid with a black interviewer. This was particularly true of the black men who had raped white women. They told me they found it difficult to discuss their rapes with me because their victims had been white—a fact they expected would particularly upset or anger another white woman. I tried to assure them that the race of their victims did not make their crimes any better or worse. Still, their embarrassment affected the interviews, and my impression is that Joe was a more successful interviewer in these cases. Hindsight suggests that the ideal gender and race combination for this research would have been a black woman and a white woman.

13 This technique is similar to what others have used in prison research. See Athens (1977), Luckenbill (1977), and Queen's Bench Foundation (1978).

14 Presentence reports are written by court workers at the time of conviction and, although the quality varies, usually include general background information, a psychological evaluation, the offender's version of the details of the crime, and the victim's or police's version of the details of the crime.

15 It is theoretically possible that some, but certainly not all, of these men were innocent. However, even if that were true, there is no way to establish such a fact and, additionally, the purpose of the research was not to overturn convictions or to pry confessions out of participants. Instead, it is necessary to assume that, as judge or jury determined, they are guilty as charged.

2

Rape Is the Problem

Sunny afternoon
chase away my blues
start me thinking
of the times
I spent with you
     Summer days
     the midnight waves . . .
I'M GOING TO RAPE YOU
going to ripe [sic] off you dress
make your life a mess
I'M GOING TO RAPE YOU
In the ally [sic] by the store
I'll be waiting at the door
I'M GOING TO RAPE YOU
turn you into a little whore
when I'm done you'll beg for more
I'M GOING TO . . .
I'M GOING TO RAPE YOUR BODY . . . YOUR MIND . . .
     YOUR SOUL
    No one will claim they knew ya
    even your husband
I'M GOING TO RAPE YOU
        (anonymous—found pasted on a storefront)

Rape as Women's Problem

Sparked by the efforts of concerned women, during the
decade of the 1970s, rape was "discovered." This period

33

witnessed heightened media attention to the victimization of women as well as a growing body of rape literature in both the popular and the scholarly press. Women's groups mobilized to educate the public and to assist the victims of rape. A number of states yielded to the pressure of the women's movement and revised rape statutes that had been insensitive to the rights of rape victims. In Washington, D.C., a national center, established and funded by Congress, was mandated to direct efforts toward the prevention and control of rape. Indeed, a serious social problem, no stranger to women, had been identified. Yet, despite this enlightenment and the passing of two decades, rape remains firmly embedded in the public regard as a "women's problem."

Rape, of course, is a serious problem for women. Johnson (1980) employed life-table analysis to calculate the lifetime risk of rape to females aged 12 and over.[1] Excluding sexual abuse in marriage and assuming all women are equally at risk,[2] if rape rates remain unchanged, Johnson conservatively estimates that 20 to 30 percent of girls now 12 years old will suffer a violent sexual attack during the remainder of their lives. Although Johnson's estimate has been criticized as too high (Gollin 1980), another recent prediction, based on an independent data source, suggests his estimate may be accurate. Again, assuming no future change in rape rates, Russell and Howell (1983) estimate that there is at least a 26 percent probability that a woman living in San Francisco will become the victim of a completed rape at some time in her life (see also Russell 1982). Additionally, they estimate there is a 46 percent probability that she will be victimized by a completed rape or attempted rape during her lifetime.[3]

These estimates, which demonstrate the frightening frequency of sexual violence in the United States, suggest that a critical examination of popular explanations for rape is in order. Johnson (1980) makes a similar observation as he questions how responsibility for such a common occurrence can rest solely with a "small lunatic fringe of psychopathic men." Instead, he argues, "the numbers reiterate a reality that American women have lived with for years: sexual violence against women is part of the everyday fabric of American life" (p. 146).

The research reported in this book also challenges the assumption that individual psychopathology is the predisposing factor that best explains the majority of sexual violence against women. Instead, the position taken here is that psychopathology, or the "disease" model, is too limited an explanation, which, by focusing on "sickness," ignores ample evidence that links sexual aggression to cultural factors and suggests that rape, like all behavior, is learned and, from the actors' perspective, serves a purpose. This is important because the disease model has retarded efforts to arrive at a general explanation for sexual violence and, ultimately, has narrowed our perception of rape to that of a "women's problem" to avoid rather than a "men's problem" to end.

The Medicalization of Rape

Rape is only one of several social problems (like alcoholism, drug use, and gambling) that has been medicalized over the past several decades (for example, see Conrad and Schneider 1980). Indeed, in the case of rape, psychiatry dominated the literature for 50 years. Because members of the medical profession are widely regarded as experts, they have been relatively free to define problems, like rape, from their own perspective. As behaviors like rape came to be viewed as caused by disease—that is, as having origins in biogenic factors—medicine increasingly came to be viewed as the legitimate agent of social control. Thus, the medical profession acquired the power to designate appropriate treatments and interventions that also depended on medicine for implementation. The rise of sexual psychopathy legislation is a good example of the general trend toward the medicalization of deviant behavior.

By 1965, under the influence of psychiatry, 30 states and the District of Columbia had sexual psychopath laws, which generally define a rapist in sexual terms as "a person unable to control his sexual impulse or having to commit sex crimes" (Bowman and Engle 1965). As the expert on sexual psychopathy, psychiatry became an integral part of the legal process. However, critics argue that the sexual psychopath designation "subsumes a long, broadly descriptive list of personality traits and is not a specific diagnostic label based on scientific data" (Bowman and Engle 1965, 766). They point out that legal definitions mixed with psychiatric terms have proven to be administratively ineffective. Research has demonstrated, for example, that individuals who would be defined as having more serious emotional disturbances quite often commit minor offenses, and vice versa (Ellis and Brancale 1956). Other research points to the observation that psychiatrists frequently disagree with each others' expert testimony and suggests that diagnostic findings often depend upon which side of a case has engaged the expert (for a review, see Simon and Zusman 1983). Some psychiatrists also are critical of the idea of a sexual psychopath and, in 1977, the Group for the Advancement of Psychiatry, with a membership of some 300 psychiatrists, called for the repeal of sexual psychopath legislation. After an extensive study and evaluation, the group's Committee on Psychiatry and the Law (1977) concluded that sexual psychopath statutes are approaches that have failed, that the categorization process projected by these statutes lacks clinical validity, and that predictions about "sexual dangerousness" are unreliable.

Despite these criticisms, psychiatry moved from an advisory position to one in which the profession exercised control over the labeling and, consequently, the sentencing and release of sex offenders. To accomplish this, psychiatry claimed a professional monopoly over a body of expert knowledge. Once the idea of sexual psychopathology had been established, the profession also could claim that medicine held the solution. Over the past 50 years, to varying degrees, medicine has experimented with castration, psychosurgery, electric shock, and hormonal and mind-control drug therapy, as well as psychotherapy, all in the name of rape prevention and control.[4] And although men who rape are not confined to one social class, the object of these "therapies" generally has been lower-status men who lack the means to protect themselves from the more intrusive forms of treatment. But while the debate over medicine's role and effectiveness in law continues, psychiatry remains firmly entrenched in the legal process.

Is Rape a Disease?

The psychopathological perspective is one of a number of ways in which human behavior, including sexual violence, can be conceptualized. However, in the case of sexual violence, until recently, the assumptions of psychopathology have been at the core of most research on rapists and the elements emphasized in the disease model became the popularly accepted explanations for why men rape.

At the core of the disease model are essentially two assumptions: that rape is the result of a mental illness, and that it often includes an uncontrollable sexual impulse.[5] The assertion is that men who rape lack the ability to control themselves and that they are "sick," disordered individuals. Especially in the early psychoanalytic literature, rapists were often described as suffering from a disease that weakened their self-control and created an "irresistible impulse" to commit a sexual act. Thus, rape was viewed as the "explosive expression of a pent up impulse" (Guttmacher and Weinhofen 1952, 116). Clearly, since men who rape could not control their behavior, they were not responsible for it either.

Despite historically widespread usage in psychiatric litera-ture, impulse theory lacks empirical support. No one has been able to demonstrate that men who rape are more or less prone to impulsive behavior than other known groups of men. In fact, if anything, research has demonstrated the opposite of impulse theory. For example, Amir (1971) analyzed the police records of 646 rapes and found that 71 percent were premeditated, not sudden, impulsive acts. Hypothetically, impulse theory could be used to explain any behavior, and if the courts extended the logic of irresistible impulse to its limits, no one would be responsible for anything. It has, however, been used primarily to explain rape and other forms of sexual violence. Certainly the idea of an uncontrollable male sex urge fits the traditional image of a naturally boundless and untamable male sex drive, in contrast to the natural passivity of women (see Scully and Bart 1973; also, Scully 1980).

Irresistible impulse does not necessarily imply a character disorder, but when rape is viewed as a disease, it does suggest a sex act perpetrated by a perverted and sick individual. For example, Littner (1973, 7) states, "The single most important item we need to know about the sex offender is how sick he is emotionally. This is far more important than the nature of the crime he has committed." Likewise, Karpman (1951, 190) has argued that "sexual psychopaths are, of course, a social menace, but they are not conscious agents deliberately and viciously perpetrating these acts, rather they are the victims of a disease from which many suffer more than their victims." Given the presumption of illness, many psychiatrists concluded that rape is merely symptomatic of the real disease or underlying disorder. And frequently in the older literature, the psychiatric shibboleths of homosexuality and hostility toward a mother figure (to be discussed in Chapter 3) were conjured up to explain the hidden motive.

Inasmuch as medicine's major paradigm is pathology, it is not surprising that some psychiatrists perceive the world in such terms. But to understand the application of psychopathology to rape in particular, it is also necessary to look at the type of man typically available to therapists. As pointed out in Chapter 1, conclusions typically are based on small numbers of rapists selected from the therapists' own patient population in prison. Generally, these men admit to themselves and others that they have raped, and they seek therapy in prison to discover whether emotional problems caused their behavior. While their desire for help may be genuine, they are also aware that a positive psychiatric evaluation is paramount for parole. Thus, not only is the relationship between therapist and client unscientific, but the men studied represent only a small proportion of convicted rapists, since many men deny both rape and emotional problems, and they may be even less representative of men outside of prison who rape but are able to avoid detection and/or conviction.

The belief in disease as a causal explanation for rape has been amazingly persistent despite the relative lack of empirical support for such a view. For example, research-oriented clinical psychologists have concentrated on distinguishing rapists from nonrapists on the basis of projective and other personality tests. Hammer and Jacks (1955) found that the Rorschach test distinguished between rapists, characterized by an aggressive behavioral orientation, and pedophiles, characterized by a passive-submissive behavioral orientation. However, attempts to use the Rorschach test to distinguish between rapists and "normals," and between rapists and men convicted of aggressive nonsexual crimes, have not revealed significant differences.

Rada (1978), summarizing several studies of rapists utilizing the Minnesota Multiphasic Personality Inventory (MMPI), states that the MMPI composite profile of rapists sometimes shows elevation in the psychopath deviate scale. However, he also cautions that individual rapists often show markedly different MMPI profiles from the composite profile. Recently, a group of researchers at the Clarke Institute of Psychiatry in Toronto administered the MMPI to 40 nonviolent sex offenders (exhibitionists and voyeurs), 40 normal controls, 25 nonsexual assaultive offenders (charged with common assault), and 40 admitted rapists who were undergoing pretrial evaluations at the Clarke Institute (Langevin et al. 1985). They found that rapists and nonsexual assaulters were most similar in that "both groups tended to be depressed, suspicious, ruminating, worrying, confused, and higher in energy compared to the nonassaultive groups" (pp. 23–24). Rapists, they report, were more feminine, somewhat less energetic, more introverted, and less paranoid than assaulters. On the basis of these characteristics, they conclude, "the two assaultive groups had a wide range of symptoms reflecting strong emotional disturbance" (p. 23). The implication, that these "symptoms" are somehow causally linked to rape and/or aggressive behavior, bears closer scrutiny. That is, it is equally valid to suggest that these "symptoms" may be the effect (not the cause) of the situation these men now find themselves in—arrested, charged with a serious crime, and in a psychiatric hospital awaiting a trial that could result in long years of prison. Under these circumstances, one might question the emotional health of a person who did not tend to be depressed, suspicious, ruminating, worried, confused, and withdrawn!

Several attempts have been made to assess sex offenders' sexual behavior through psychological testing (see Cowden and Pacht 1969; Thore and Haupt 1966). The value of much of this research is limited because rapists were not examined as a separate category of sex offender. In one study, however, 100 rapists were administered the Edwards Personal Preference Schedule (Fisher and Rivlin 1971). In contrast to findings on Rorschach testing, compared to normals, rapists tended to be less aggressive, less independent and self-motivated, and less self-assured and dominant. The authors suggest that these findings are consistent with the view that rape is an expression of hostility by a male who feels weak, inadequate, and dependent. They do not explain, however, why women are used as the object upon which this hostility is vented.

There are somewhat more consistent findings, though fewer studies, on hostility among rapists. Replicating his own previous research, Rada (1978, 31) administered the Buss-Durke Hostility Inventory to 10 brutally violent rapists, 10 nonviolent rapists, and 20 nonviolent child molesters. He found that while all three groups scored above normals, the brutally violent rapists scored higher than the other two groups of sex offenders.

In summary, the psychological research on rapists can be characterized as inconsistent and inconclusive. Part of the problem is methodological. Some studies suffer from inadequate sample size. Because of difficulty in obtaining subjects, very small numbers are typical in rape research. Other studies fail to differentiate between rapists and other groups who are collectively labeled sex offenders, including pedophiles, voyeurs, exhibitionists, and even gay males, historically regarded as exhibiting pathology in their sexual preference. Choice of control groups reflects a related methodological problem also connected to the disease model: the assumption that the most appropriate comparisons are between categories of sex offenders rather than between rapists and other heterosexual men whose sexual preference is adult women. (Interestingly, however, when rapists are compared to other sex offenders, some studies have concluded that rapists are the "healthiest" subgroup of the sex offender category; see Albin 1977.) Additionally, psychological tests are administered after, not before, the act, making it unclear whether those patterns that do emerge are related to the behavior or are the effect of the individual's current situation, or are neither. This problem is unavoidable, but the failure to distinguish between correlation and causality in much of the research on rapists is avoidable. That is, the fact that two observations occur together does not necessarily mean that one is causing the other. From a sociological perspective, these studies also tell us nothing about how the sexually violent behavior comes to be actualized: why all men with similar personality traits do not rape. Rada (1978) suggests that the relative lack of psychological studies in the past decade may be due to dissatisfaction with the techniques and the inability to correlate personality factors with specific criminal behaviors.

Some men who rape, like some people who steal, undeniably are mentally ill. In the case of rape, however, empirical studies indicate that only as few as 5 percent of men are psychotic at the time of their crimes (Abel et al. 1980), fairly strong evidence that psychopathology does not explain the vast amount of sexually violent behavior. The problem is with absolute statements such as the claim, made by one psychiatrist, that "I have never studied a rapist where there was not present, together with many other problems, a rather severe sexual disorder" (quoted in Albin 1977, 431). The presumption of psychopathology is also evident in the often-cited work of Groth (1979), a prison psychologist. While Groth emphasizes the nonsexual nature of rape—power, anger, and sadism—he also concludes, "Rape is always a symptom of some psychological dysfunction, either temporary and transient or chronic and repetitive" (p. 5). Before considering the implications of these explanations, there is one other major theme—victim precipitated rape—that deserves attention.

Blaming the Victim

Traditionally, support for the allegation that women precipitate rape came from victimology, a subfield of criminology, in which the victim's contribution to the genesis of crime was the subject of study. Recently, victimology has also focused on crime from the victim's perspective.

Criminologist Hans von Hentig was one of the first to articulate the victimologists' position. In a work published

41

in 1940, he states that "the human victim in many instances seems to lead the evildoer actively into temptation. The predator is—by varying means—prevailed to advance against the prey" (p. 303). If there are born criminals, he argues, there are born victims, who are self-harming and self-destructive. Central to his thesis is the question of why a specific victim is chosen. In the case of incest and rape, according to von Hentig, seduction plays a prominent role, leading him to question whether rape may not be considered a case of "the oversexed on the oversexed" (p. 209).

The work of sociologist Menachem Amir is a more contemporary example of the application of victimology to rape. Amir (1972) makes a distinction between victim-precipitating behaviors through acts of *commission* and through acts of *omission*. Commissive behavior includes "last moment retreating from sexual advancement" or "agreeing voluntarily to drink or ride with a stranger" (p. 155). Acts of omission include failure to take preventive measures, such as failing to react strongly enough to sexual suggestions, or "when her outside appearance arouses the offender's advances which are not staved off" (p. 155). Amir states that, under these circumstances, "the victim becomes functionally responsible for the offense by entering upon and following a course that will provoke some males to commit crimes" (p. 155). Thus Amir argues that attention should be focused upon the victim-offender relationship, the moral character of the victim, and the "victim's personality makeup which may orient her toward the offender and the offense" (p. 132). While the field of victimology can be accused of overidentifying with offenders, in the case of rape, psychoanalytic theory provided the theoretical basis that could be used to discredit victims.

In psychoanalytic terms, the core female personality consists of three characteristics: narcissism, masochism, and passivity. The masochistic element accounts for women's alleged unconscious desire to be raped. In her summary of the psychoanalytic view of the female personality, Horney (1973, 24) states:

The specific satisfactions sought and found in female sex life and motherhood are of a masochistic nature. The

42

content of the early sexual wishes and fantasies concerning the father is the desire to be mutilated, that is castrated by him. Menstruation has the hidden connotation of a masochistic experience. What the woman secretly desires in intercourse is rape and violence, or in the mental sphere, humiliation. . . . This swinging in the direction of masochism is part of the woman's anatomical destiny.

While the psychoanalytic view of women has been widely criticized for its obvious bias (for example, see Chesler 1972), with the exception of Albin (1977), no one has noted how easily it can be translated into a rationalization for male sexual aggressive behavior.

In the psychoanalytic literature, victims of sexual violence have frequently been sorted into categories on the basis of personal or circumstantial characteristics. Littner (1973, 23), for example, distinguishes between "true victims," those who do not consciously or unconsciously wish to be raped, and "professional victims," those who have an inner masochistic need to be raped. According to Littner, "professional victims" have an inner need to be sexually molested or attacked even though consciously they are totally unaware of their motivation. Because of these unconscious desires, they "unwittingly cooperate with the rapist in terms of covertly making themselves available to the rapist" (p. 28). It is perhaps unnecessary to point out that the victims of other types of crimes are rarely alleged to have an inner need to be victimized, nor are they routinely accused of causing the crimes committed against them.

In some psychoanalytic literature, not only victims and mothers, but also the wives of rapists have been held responsible for their husbands' sexual violence. Abrahamsen (1960, 163), in his discussion of eight wives who had been subjected to sexual aggression by their rapist husbands, states, "The offender needs an outlet for his sexual aggression and finds a submissive partner who unconsciously invites sexual abuse and whose masochistic needs are being fulfilled." The fact that these women had divorced their rapist-husbands did not alter Abrahamsen's belief in the psychoanalytic model. Instead, he argues that the wives were also latently aggressive and competitive. In Abrahamsen's scheme, the rapist-husband was the innocent victim of his wife, his mother, and the woman he raped. He emphatically states:

> There can be *no doubt* that the sexual frustration which the *wives* caused is one of the factors motivating the rape which might be tentatively described as a displaced attempt to force a *seductive but rejecting mother* into submission. The sex offender was not only exposed to his *wife's masculine and competitive inclinations*, but also, in a certain sense, was somehow *seduced* into committing the crime. (p. 165; emphasis added)

Perhaps even more perplexing than the treatment of women is what has been said about girls who are the victims of rape and/or incest. Girls have been alleged to have the same subconscious motives as their adult counterparts. For example, Abrahamsen presents the thesis that sexual trauma is often unconsciously desired by the child and that it represents a form of infantile sexual activity. He states:

> If there is an underlying unconscious wish for it, the experiencing of sexual trauma in childhood is a masochistic expression of the sexual impulse. . . . We can say that children belonging to this category show an abnormal desire for obtaining sexual pleasure and, in the consequence of this, undergo sexual trauma. (p. 54)

"Research" that incorporated this perspective typically blamed children for the behavior of their adult molesters. For example, a frequently quoted study of girls who were the victims of adult sex offenders distinguished between "accidental" victims and "participating" victims, "those who took part in the initiating and maintaining of the relationship" (Weiss et al. 1955). Half, or 23 out of 44, of the victims labeled as "participating" were under age 10, and some were as young as 4 or 5 years old. Furthermore, "participation" was determined on the basis of psychiatric evaluations of the victims' personalities rather than on the objective facts of the cases. Weiss et al. conclude that the girls had severe emotional problems that motivated their initiation and participation in their own victimization. These psychiatrists apparently never even considered the possibility that the girls' problems might be the result, not the cause, of the rape or incest. Elsewhere in the literature, girl victims have been described as very attractive, charming, appealing, submissive, and seductive, even though some were as young as 4 years old (see Bender 1965).

Boys as well as girls are sexually victimized. However, discussions of male victimization traditionally have lacked the suggestion that victim precipitation is the root of the problem. For example, Halleck (1965) states, "Most girl victims are familiar with the offender and many are willing or passive participants in the sexual act." About males, he states, "A significant number of male victims may be considered truly 'accidental' in the sense that they did not know the attacker and did not willingly participate in the act" (p. 680).

Why Isn't Rape Men's Problem?

The studies that have been discussed above span four decades—the 1940s through the 1970s—and have been influential in shaping our thinking about rape in very important ways. Each of the explanations—irresistible impulse, disease, and victim precipitation—embraces a view of rape that has several implications. First, each explanation absolves the offender of responsibility for his behavior. When rape is viewed as a disease, it casts the offender in the sick role. Behavior attributed to an incapacity beyond the individual's control carries an obligation to admit illness and seek medical help. The idea that women consciously or subconsciously precipitate their own victimization has a similar consequence. Attention is focused on the behavior and motives of the victim rather than on the offender. Thus, responsibility is also shifted to the victim. The assumptions that underscore allegations of victim-precipitated rape are also a clear example of the way ideology shapes theory and thus research, despite claims of objectivity. There is little doubt whose interests are served by these supposedly scientifically neutral formulations. And the influence of this ideology extends well beyond scholarly journals. As numerous observers have noted, in court, it is often the rape victim who is on trial.

Second, psychopathological explanations make the assumption that male aggressive sexual behavior is unusual or strange. Thus, sexual violence is removed from the realm of the everyday or "normal" world and placed in the category of "special" behavior. As a result, sexually violent men are cast as outsiders, and any connection or threat to "normal" men is eliminated.

Third, and perhaps most salient, the psychopathological model views rape as no more than a collection of individualistic, idiosyncratic problems. This creates the tendency to look for the cause of and solution to a complex social problem within the individual and to ignore the cultural and structural context in which it occurs. The net effect of individualistic explanations is to create an approach to the problem that never reaches beyond the individual offender. When sexually violent behavior is presumed to be confined to a few "sick" men, the solution becomes to use drugs, surgery, shock therapy, or psychotherapy to "cure" those few individuals who are causing the problem. Women can help to prevent "their problem" by avoiding contact with this "lunatic fringe." Thus the psychopathological model of rape removes the necessity of investigating or changing those elements within a society that may precipitate sexual violence against women. The consequence of defining responsibility this way is that men never have to confront rape as their problem. After all, either men who rape are defective or the real culprits are women. In a society where status and power belong to men, such an ideology is not unexpected.

The psychopathological model, developed by a profession dominated by men, is a prime example of reductionist thinking in which androcentric blinders diminish a complex social problem to a singular simplistic cause. At worst, the model blames the victim; at best, it leaves the vast majority of sexual violence unexplained. Additionally, the psychopathological model does not explain why women in some societies are the targets of so much uniquely male "disease." To do it justice, the parameters of the problem must be broadened to incorporate new perspectives and behavioral theories. The competing feminist model embraces culture and social structure as dynamic and contributing factors and takes an alternative multifaceted view of sexual violence and its origins.

Culture's Contribution

Anthropological data provide insight (albeit limited) into the cultural antecedents of rape in preindustrial tribal societies. In one study, using Murdock and White's Standard Cross-Cultural Sample, researchers determined that of the 34 groups for which frequency could be established, rape was absent in 8, rare in 12, and common in 14 societies (Broude and Greene 1976). Sanday (1979), using an altered coding scheme and additional sources, found a larger number of societies in which rape appears to be absent or rare—44 out of 95 tribal groups. Despite these discrepant numbers, ethnographic data do establish the existence of rape-free preindustrial societies.[6] The absence of rape in some societies provides support for the proposition that while human behavior, including sexual behavior, may have biological or physiological components, it is always patterned and expressed in cultural terms.

Taking her analysis a step further, Sanday examined differences between "rape-free" and "rape-prone" societies. She argues that male dominance and the forcible control of women evolve as societies become more dependent on male destructive capacities than on female fertility. Thus, Sanday relates sexual violence to contempt for female qualities and suggests that rape is part of a culture of violence and expression of male dominance.

In contrast, Blumberg (1979) proposes a structural approach to the examination of women's oppression within and among different cultures. The key to her elaborate paradigm is women's degree of control over the means of production and generated surplus relative to men of the same group. Blumberg argues that women are more likely to lack important life options and to be oppressed physically and politically where they do not have any appreciable economic power. Using a pilot sample of 61 preindustrial societies from the Human Relations Area Files, Blumberg found preliminary support for her hypothesis. The higher women's relative economic power, the less likely they are to be beaten by the men in their lives. Thus, it appears that in preindustrial societies economic power enables women to win immunity from males' use of force against them. Schwendinger and Schwendinger (1983) make a similar point, arguing that rape is related to sexual inequality, women's participation in social production, and the degree to which violence is institutionalized in other aspects of the culture. To summarize, anthropological research suggests that sexual violence is related to cultural attitudes, the power relationship between women and men, the social and economic status of women relative to the men of their group, and the amount of other forms of violence in the society.

While there may be no example of a rape-free modern culture, the frequency of rape varies dramatically among societies, and the United States is among the most rape-prone of all. In 1980, for example, the rate of reported rape and attempted rape for the United States was 18 times higher than the corresponding rate for England and Wales (West 1983), leading Griffin (1971) to call rape "the All-American crime."

The All-American Crime

In feminist theory rape is viewed as a singularly male form of sexual coercion—an act of violence and social control that functions to "keep women in their place." The justification for forced sexual access is buttressed by legal, social, and religious definitions of women as inferior male property and sex as an exchange of goods (for example, see Brownmiller 1975; Clark and Lewis 1977; Griffin 1979; Russell 1975). MacKinnon (1987) asserts that legal definitions of rape are based on what men, not women, think violates women. From women's point of view, MacKinnon (1983) argues, rape is not prohibited, it is regulated. Bart (1979) refers to rape as a paradigm of sexism. She notes that definitions, notably legal definitions, reflect the belief system of the dominant

48

group. Therefore, she argues, it is not by accident that the *de facto* and *de jure* definitions of rape embody sexist beliefs; for example, intercourse forced on a wife by her husband is not rape. Indeed, a number of feminists have observed that rape laws and the corresponding penalties are not intended to protect women as much as they are intended to protect men's property, which, having been damaged, loses market value (for example, see LeGrand 1973; MacKinnon 1987).

In feminist theory rape is related to the power relationship between men and women, which, Lipman-Blumen (1984) argues, is at the very core of our social fabric and forms the blueprint for all other power relationships. Hanmer and Maynard (1987) conclude that recent feminist research reveals the existence of a complex social structure where power, inequality, and oppression function along socially constructed gender lines and, in this system, violence is used to control women. In this sense, feminist theorists have pointed out that, because it preserves male dominance, sexual violence benefits all men, not just those who actually rape. Systematic gender-based stratification is sustained through social, legal, economic, political, and social institutional supports. Women don't revolt, Lipman-Blumen asserts, because both genders have been taught through "control myths" to believe that female/male differences are innate. In her view, two "control myths" in particular are important—that men are more capable and knowledgeable than women and that men have women's best interests at heart (colonialism revisited). These "control myths" not only prevent women from gaining access to institutional resources—which, as Blumberg (1979) points out, is critical to gaining immunity from male sexual violence—but they also contribute to a social climate in which women often are not believed when they say they have been raped.

Feminist theorists view rape as an extension of norma- tive male behavior, the result of conformity to the values and prerogatives that define the male role in patriarchal societies. Crucial are the "control myths" that teach the innate superiority of men and the corresponding inferiority of women. Equally important are socialization practices that teach men to have expectations about their level of sexual needs and corresponding female accessibility, which functions to justify forcing sexual access. Weis and Borges (1973) point out that socialization prepares women to be "legitimate" victims and men to be potential offenders. Herman (1984) concludes that the United States is a rape culture because both genders are taught to regard male aggression as a natural and normal part of sexual relations.

The Boy Next Door

Early feminist literature, Anne Edwards (1987) points out, tended to approach various types of male violence as discrete behavioral categories. With theoretical maturity, however, sexual aggression/violence is now conceptualized as a continuum or series of behaviors ranging from verbal street harassment and harassment in the workplace to wife battering, incest, and rape—connected by the common underlying function of the systematic control of women (for example, see Kelly 1987). Likewise, men can be thought of as varying along a continuum of sexual aggression, with some men more likely than others to commit aggressive acts against women. Striking evidence for this proposition is found in a growing body of research that indicates that many men in this society are capable of sexual aggression.

Koss and Leonard (1984) adopted the continuum approach to measure the amount of "hidden" rape in a normal population. Their measurement varies the degree to which aggression has been used on a female partner to accomplish intercourse and distinguishes among four categories: (1) sexually assaultive—admits to obtaining vaginal, oral, or anal intercourse through the threat or use of force (legally rape in most states); (2) sexually abusive—admits to some degree of force or use of force but intercourse did not take place (attempted rape in most states); (3) sexually coercive—admits to obtaining intercourse with an unwilling woman by threatening to end the relationship, by lying about feelings (false statements of love and so on), or after continual arguments; (4) sexually nonaggressive—admits to none of the categories. In their sample of 1,846 college males, 4.3 percent reported sexually assaultive behavior; 4.9 percent, sexually abusive behavior; 22.4 percent, sexually coercive behavior; and 59.0 percent reported no sexually aggressive behavior but did report mutually desired sexual experiences. Finally, 9.4 percent of the males reported no sexual experience of any kind. Extending this research to a national sample of 6,159 male and female students enrolled in 32 colleges and universities across the United States, Koss et al. (1987) found that 53.7 percent of women respondents indicated some form of sexual victimization since age 14, including the following: sexual contact, 14.4 percent; sexual coercion, 11.9 percent; attempted rape, 12.1 percent; and rape, 15.4 percent (categorized by most serious event). Among male students, 25.1 percent revealed involvement in some form of sexual aggression, including the following: sexual contact, 10.2 percent; sexual coercion, 7.2 percent; attempted rape, 3.3 percent; and rape, 4.4 percent (categorized by most serious act). These findings are consistent with research reported by Kirkpatrick and Kanin (1957) conducted during the mid-1950s on college women (see also Kanin 1957, 1965, 1967, 1969, 1970). In their sample of 291 women, they found 56 percent reported offensive experiences at some level of erotic intimacy, including 21 percent who had been offended by "forceful attempts at sexual intercourse" and 6 percent who had experienced "aggressively forceful attempts at sexual intercourse in the course of which menacing threats or coercive infliction of physical pain were employed." The authors conclude that sexual aggression is commonplace in dating relationships.

Equally disturbing are the findings of research designed to gauge sexual aggression in a normal population by asking men to rate their own likelihood of raping if they are assured they would not be caught. Replicating earlier research by Malamuth, Haber, and Feshbach (1980), Briere and Malamuth (1983) found that out of 356 college men, 28 percent indicated some likelihood of both raping and using force, 6 percent some likelihood of rape but not force, 30 percent some likelihood of force but not rape, and 40 percent no likelihood of either rape or force. A second purpose of their research was to gather data on the two competing theories of rape: that rape is a form of sexual psychopathy committed by men who cannot control their sexual impulses versus the sociocultural

explanation, that rape is the logical extension of a male dominant–female submissive gender role stereotyped culture. They
found that self-reported potential willingness to be sexually
aggressive was unrelated to a variety of sexual variables.
However, in support of the sociocultural explanation, they
found that rape-supportive attitudes and beliefs did predict
likelihood to rape or to use sexual aggression.

In similar but unrelated research, Tieger (1981) obtained
results highly compatible with those of Briere and Malamuth.
In Tieger's sample of 172 college males, 37 percent indicated
some likelihood of raping if assured of not being caught;
20 percent indicated a likelihood greater than or equal to
the midpoint of the rating scale ("somewhat") that they
themselves would rape (labeled HLR). Compared to non-HLR
males, analysis of the HLR group revealed a greater degree of
belief that rape victims act seductively and enjoy being raped,
and that other males are also likely to rape. The HLR males
were also more likely than non-HLR males to view rape as
a less serious crime, and they held a more sympathetic view
toward rapists.

Quite clearly, self-reports of college males and victim reports
reveal that sexual aggression is commonplace in college dating
relationships. An even larger number of college males express
willingness to rape or sexually aggress against women given
the absence of a penalty. Indeed, in their research, Martin and
Hummer (1989) found that college fraternities, in particular,
create an environment in which the use of coercion in sexual
relationships with women is regarded as normal. If such
patterns are found in college populations, there is every reason
to believe the situation is similar in non-college-educated
populations. Finally, callous attitudes toward women and
belief in rape myths are the most consistent predictors of
male sexual aggression.

In light of these findings, it is important to comment, at
least briefly, on typical campus rape prevention strategies.
Precautions such as increased lighting and escort services
are premised on the assumption that the greatest threat to
women is a psychotic stranger. The media, it should be
pointed out, contribute to this image by focusing so much
print and airtime on spectacular and unusual criminals when,

in fact, those offenders are responsible for only a small proportion of crime. Indeed, contrary to popular wisdom, a long history of data clearly indicate that college women are at greater risk of being raped or aggressed against by the men they know and date than they are by lunatics in the bushes, yet little is done to prevent the more common occurrence. As I will argue frequently in this book, theories of causation are important because they beget strategies for prevention.

Pornography and the Normalization of Rape

Considerable evidence supports the observation that sexual violence has been so trivialized in the United States that rape has come to be regarded as normal and acceptable under certain conditions. The widely publicized 1983 rape of a woman who went to Big Dan's Bar in New Bedford, Massachusetts, to buy a pack of cigarettes is but one example. In this ordeal, which lasted more than two hours, several Portuguese men raped a young Portuguese woman on a pool table while other men prevented the bartender from calling the police and cheered the attackers on. While the closely knit Portuguese community initially reacted with shock and sympathy for the victim, within a brief span of time the situation changed to one of hostility toward the victim and sympathy for the rapists, whose actions were justified as appropriate under the circumstances. Both men and women in the community, in part to counter the anti-Portuguese sentiment provoked by the notoriety of the case, attempted to neutralize the crime by blaming the victim for being in the bar at night alone while her children were left unattended at home (for a full analysis, see Chancer 1987). Said one woman, "They did nothing to her. Her rights are to be home with her two kids and to be a good mother. A Portuguese woman should be home with her kids and that's it" (quoted in Chancer 1987, 251) and 16,000 people signed petitions asking for leniency for the rapists (p. 251).

Many feminists and others point to the growing accessibility of violent and degrading pornography as one (but

53

certainly not the only) of the more potent nourishers of a cultural climate that accepts sexual violence.[7] A critical issue is the nature and direction of the relationship between violent, degrading pornography and sexual aggression. In this chapter, the research on pornography's role in the trivialization of rape will be explored; in a later chapter, the effect of violent pornography on male aggression will be examined.

Advocates of pornography typically refer to several sources of data as evidence that pornography has no antisocial effect and may even be beneficial. Often quoted are the Denmark studies (see Ben-Veniste 1971; Kutchinsky 1971), which seem to indicate a relationship between a reduction in sexually related crimes and the lifting of legal restrictions on pornography. Based in part on the Danish data, the 1970 U.S. Commission on Obscenity and Pornography issued what became a highly controversial conclusion—that no relationship, positive or negative, exists between pornography and sexual offenses. Others, however, challenged the 1970 commission's conclusion (see Bart and Jozsa 1980).

Court (1984), in an extensive review of the studies considered by the 1970 commission, points to a number of problems. He argues that the use of sex crimes as an index of effect is open to confusing and conflicting interpretations. Not only are there problems with underreporting of these crimes, but, Court observes, one must distinguish between *major* and *minor* sexual offenses, since the trends for these do not correlate well. HHis and others' data indicate that reports of minor sexual offenses (e.g., carnal knowledge, voyeurism) have generally declined in Denmark and elsewhere over the past decade, whereas reports of more serious offenses, such as rape, have increased. He points out, "Since the minor offenses are cumulatively greater in number than the major offenses, it follows that a reduction in the former will result in the aggregated total giving false reassurance about trends by masking an increase in serious offenses" (p. 148). Therefore, he insists, if anything is to be concluded about the effect of violent pornography from crime trends, it is minimally necessary to distinguish between sex crimes that include elements of violence, like rape and attempted rape, and sex offenses, like peeping and exhibitionism, that are nonviolent. The latter offenses are not relevant to the pornography debate.

The debate over pornography was reopened on the federal level when, in 1985, Attorney General William French Smith established the 1985 Attorney General's Commission on Pornography.[8] The commission's mandate was broad: "to determine the nature, extent, and impact on society of pornography in the United States, and to make specific recommendations to the then current Attorney General, Edwin Meese, concerning effective ways in which the spread of pornography could be contained, consistent with constitutional guarantees" (Attorney General's Commission on Pornography 1986). The findings of the 1985 commission differed markedly from those of the earlier commission, and, while hailed by many, the 1985 commission's report also has been criticized by some as too sweeping in its conclusions about the harmfulness of various types of pornography.[9]

A number of important factors distinguish the deliberations of the 1985 commission from those of the 1970 commission. Among the more salient is the relatively large amount of research that was conducted on pornography in the years that intervened between the two investigations, thus giving the 1985 commission the advantage of more data upon which to base its conclusions. Also important, the 1985 commission included violent and degrading pornography, including child pornography, in its investigation, while the 1970 commission excluded these materials. Finally, feminists had a voice in the 1985 commission deliberations, whereas in 1970 the second wave of feminism was at an early stage of reemergence.

Of concern to many feminists (for example, see Dworkin 1980) is not sexual explicitness, but rather the profusion of degrading images of women as well as the increasing amount and degree of violence that has appeared in pornography since the 1970s (see Malamuth and Spinner 1980; Slade 1984). Not only is sex increasingly fused with violence, but, equally alarming, contemporary depictions often suggest that sexual violence has a positive outcome. For example, Smith (1976) content analyzed 428 "adults only" paperbacks and found that a major theme was the use of force on a woman who initially resists. However, in the end, regardless of the type

55

or amount of force used, the victim is depicted as eventually becoming aroused and, to her humiliation, responding physically.

Such depictions of women and rape convey several dangerous messages. First, the use of force and violence is presented as part of normal male-female sexual relations, thus trivializing and normalizing rape. Another message suggests that women desire and enjoy rape—that, in fact, sexual violence has positive consequences. This image has more potential for damage than the violence per se and is the characteristic that distinguishes rape from other types of violent fictional depictions. Victims are never portrayed as enjoying murder, bombings, robberies, or other crimes. Such displays seem to be reserved for the pornographic depiction of women being raped.

Evidence from research, conducted primarily on male college students, supports the premise that exposure to sexually violent pornography increases antagonistic attitudes toward women and intensifies belief in rape myths, particularly that victims are responsible for rape and that women are aroused by sexual violence. For example, in one in a varied series of laboratory experiments, Malamuth and Check (1985) exposed male college students to one of eight pornographic audiotapes in which the content—a woman's consent, her pain, and the outcome (her arousal versus disgust)—were systematically manipulated. Later, the men listened to a second passage depicting either consenting or nonconsenting sex. Afterwards, a series of questions and scales were used to measure the men's perceptions of the second passage and their belief in rape myths. The researchers state that their findings from this series of experiments support the hypothesis that media depictions suggesting that rape results in the victim's arousal can contribute to men's belief in a similar rape myth. Further, they found that it is men with relatively higher inclinations to aggress against women (as measured by a pretest likelihood of raping scale) who are particularly likely to be affected by media depictions of rape myths.

Malamuth and Check (1981) obtained similar results in a field experiment not vulnerable to the artificiality of a laboratory setting. In this study, 271 male and female students agreed to participate in research ostensibly focused on movie ratings. Students viewed two movies, either *Swept Away* and *The Getaway* (films that portray sexual aggression and suggest positive outcome) or two neutral films. All films were viewed in a theater on campus with regular audience members who were not part of the experiment. Several days later, in class, students completed a sexual attitude survey embedded with scales measuring acceptance of interpersonal violence toward women and rape myth acceptance. Students were not aware of any connection between the survey and the films. Results indicated that exposure to the films portraying aggressive sexuality with positive consequences significantly increased male, but not female, subjects' acceptance of interpersonal violence toward women and tended to increase males' acceptance of rape myths.

Even more alarming, Linz et al. (1984) have demonstrated that the more prolonged the exposure to filmed violence, the lower the sensitivity to victims of violence in other contexts (see also Malamuth 1981a; Zillman and Bryant 1982). In their experiment, male college students were exposed to five films depicting sexuality and violence toward women—one per day, for five consecutive days. All the films had been commercially released and some had been shown on campus or on cable television and included *Texas Chainsaw Massacre*, *Maniac*, *I Spit on Your Grave*, *Vice Squad*, and *Toolbox Murders*. Over the course of the five days, the men who viewed these films came to have fewer negative emotional reactions to the films, to perceive them as significantly less violent, and to consider them considerably less degrading to women. Additionally, viewing these films affected their judgment of women in other contexts. In response to a videotaped reenactment of a complete rape trial, the men who viewed these films judged the victim to be significantly less injured and evaluated her as generally less worthy than did men in a control group who had not seen the films. It should be noted that in all these experiments, subjects were ddebriefed in an effort to erase the effects of the research on individual participants.

The results of these experiments are important because research also indicates that belief in rape myths is related to a variety of other phenomena. A number of studies have shown that strong belief in rape stereotypes results in restricted definitions of rape, not guilty verdicts in mock jury rape trials, denial or reduction of perceived injury to rape victims, and blaming rape victims for their victimization, and is a predictor of self-reported likelihood of raping (see Burt and Albin 1981; Borgida and White 1979; Calhoun et al. 1976; Jones and Aronson 1973). Further, this book will demonstrate that men convicted of rape both believe these myths and use them to justify their own sexually violent behavior.

In addition to published research, the 1985 commission listened to expert testimony at a series of six thematic public hearings held at different locations around the United States. Because of the research I was conducting on convicted rapists, I was invited to testify at the Houston, Texas, hearing, where differing opinions on the relationship between pornography and human behavior were expressed by a roster of social and behavioral scientists.[10] Essentially, I argued that research is ongoing and perhaps one day would discover a method capable of establishing whether a *causal* relationship exists between pornography and actual sexual violence against women. To do so, it will be minimally necessary to move beyond the experimental laboratory and into a broader social context. In the meantime, even in the absence of causal data, there is reason to be concerned. At the very least, we can posit an indirect relationship. That is, the more cultural support, in forms like violent and degrading pornography, that exists in a society for hostile and aggressive acts toward women, the more likely it is that such acts will occur in that society. There is ample reason to believe that these cultural supports provide the justification, if not the motivation, necessary for some men to commit sexually violent acts. Indeed, as women are only too painfully aware, the widespread availability of violent pornography in the United States has not resulted in a decrease in violent crimes against women.

Rape as Learned and Rewarding Behavior

In this investigation I apply a feminist sociocultural frame-work, predicated on a presumption of normality rather than

58

pathology, to actual men who have been convicted of rape. There is another way in which this research departs from the psychopathological tradition of men. My questions are generated from experience that women, not men, have of rape. As Harding (1987), among others, has pointed out, this is a critical distinction.

In applying a feminist sociocultural perspective to rape, I have made a number of assumptions. Starting with the observation that cultures can and do generate predispositions to behaviors that are, at the same time, defined as conditionally deviant (that is, normal deviance), I assume that rape, for the most part, is socially learned behavior. The fundamental premise is that all behavior is learned in the same way—socially through direct association with others as well as indirectly through cultural contact. Learning includes not only behavioral techniques but also a host of values and beliefs, like rape myths, that are compatible with sexual aggression against women.

Viewed this way, my approach to the men described in this book is considerably different from the bulk of previous research, which has attempted to understand why men rape by looking for evidence of pathology through an examination of individual case histories. Instead, for me, the men in this book represent a group who have reached the apex of the sexual violence continuum, a continuum that rewards men and victimizes women. They are interesting not because of their personal histories (although these collective histories are explored in Chapter 3), but because, as men who rape, they are excellent informants on our sexually violent society. Rather than assuming that rape is dysfunctional behavior, I use these informants to understand what men who rape gain from their sexually violent behavior. This approach leads to new questions about the goals men learn to achieve through sexually violent means.

But it is important to ask not only *why* but also *how* sexual violence is made possible in a society, such as ours, so prone to rape. To answer that question, it is necessary to explore the motives and rationalizations of men who rape, and their beliefs about men, women, and sexual violence in general, as well as their own victims and crimes in particular.

These will be the tasks in the pages to come. It is my hope that this exploration of men at the endpoints—admitters who do define their sexual violence as rape and deniers who do not define their sexual violence as rape—also will shed light on sexual violence at other points on the continuum.[11]

Notes

1 Johnson's (1980) estimate is based on the incidence rate for completed rapes found in the 1972 crime panel survey involving 10,000 households in 26 U.S. cities (250,000 people over age 11). The study was conducted by the Law Enforcement Assistance Administration in conjunction with the U.S. Census Bureau.

2 There are age, class, and race differences in reported rapes that suggest that all women are not equally at risk.

3 Russell and Howell (1983) applied life-table analysis to the age-specific rape rates that Russell found in a randomly selected sample of 930 adult women living in San Francisco.

4 For a full discussion of various treatments, see Rada (1978).

5 For a full discussion of the psychiatric perspective, see Scully and Marolla (1985a).

6 A number of factors limit the quantity and quality of cross-cultural data on rape. It was not customary in traditional ethnography to collect data on sexual attitudes and behavior. Further, where data do exist, they are often sketchy and vague and of questionable reliability. For these reasons, the research of Broude and Greene (1976) and Sanday (1979) do not include a number of societies found in Murdock and White's Standard Cross-Cultural Sample.

7 The issue of censorship will not be debated here. However, research linking pornography and sexual aggression is relevant to the arguments presented in this book and will be discussed.

8 The formation of the Attorney General's Commission on Pornography was announced and the eleven members named on May 20, 1985, by Edwin Meese III, who replaced William French Smith as attorney general of the United States.

9 It is not my intent here to summarize the 1,960-page report of the commission. See Attorney General's Commission on Pornography (1986).

10 The following people testified at the Houston hearing devoted to the relationship between pornography and human behavior:

- Gene Abel, professor of psychiatry, Emory University
- Paul Abramson, associate professor of psychology, UCLA

- Larry Baron, lecturer in sociology, Yale University
- Jennings Bryant, professor and chair of radio and television, University of Houston
- Don Byrne, professor and chair of psychology, SUNY—Albany
- Mary Calderone, cofounder, Sex Information and Education Council of the U.S.
- Victor Cline, professor of psychology, University of Utah
- John Court, psychologist, director of Spectrum Psychological Counseling Center
- Edward Donnerstein, professor of communication arts, University of Wisconsin—Madison
- Richard Green, professor of psychiatry, SUNY—Stony Brook
- Kathryn Kelley, associate professor of psychology, SUNY—Albany
- Neil Malamuth, professor and chair of communications, UCLA
- William Marshall, professor of psychology, Queens University, Ontario, Canada
- John Money, professor of medical psychology and pediatrics, Johns Hopkins University
- Donald Mosher, professor of psychology, University of Connecticut
- Diana Russell, professor of sociology, Mills College
- Diana Scully, associate professor of sociology, Virginia Commonwealth University
- Wendy Stock, sex therapist and assistant professor, Texas A&M University
- C. A. Tripp, psychotherapist, New York
- Ann Welbourne-Moglia, executive director, Sex Information and Education Council of the U.S.

11 As explained in Chapter 1, this is the typology that emerged naturally from the men's own perspectives on their crimes. Admitters include men who acknowledge sexual contact with their victims and also define their behavior as rape. In contrast, denier is used to refer to men who denied they had raped. Within this category, some men denied totally any involvement with their victims, while others claimed to suffer from memory loss, perhaps the ultimate denial. Most interesting is a second type of denier, men who, while they admitted sexual acts involving their victims and in some cases the use of a weapon, did not define their own behavior as rape. Much of the discussion in this book will involve distinctions between admitters and the second type of denier.

3

Profile of Convicted Rapists

A major thesis of this book is that rape is an acquired behavior, an act of normal deviance, found in societies or cultural groups whose social, economic, and political structures support sexual violence through the subordination and devaluation of women. At the same time, we also know that not all men in sexually violent societies or cultural groups rape. The task in this chapter is to develop a profile of convicted rapists and to explore what, if anything, in their backgrounds or belief systems might distinguish them from other categories of men. This profile will provide a picture of the type of man in prison for rape, who, it must be kept in mind, is more likely to fit the psychopathological model than men who rape but avoid detection or conviction. And because rapists are often presented as a special, "sicker" kind of offender, the control group of other felons, those never *convicted* of rape, will be used to identify major differences between the two groups. In general, if rapists and other felons emerge as significantly dissimilar, it will lend weight to the psychopathological explanation. However, if only minimal distinguishing characteristics are discovered, it will suggest that men who rape may not be so "special" or "different" after all.

History and Background

Each interview with the 114 convicted rapists and 75 other felons included detailed questions about childhood and family

63

experiences, marital and other relations with women, education, work, and sexual, psychological, and criminal histories. Each of the men also was given a battery of scales used to measure attitudes related to women and to sexual violence. (For a full discussion of interview form and technique, see Chapter 1.) Before each of these particulars is addressed, a quick sketch of the two groups is provided as an introduction to the men.

All of the convicted rapists discussed in this book were serving sentences for the rape or attempted rape of adult women, although several had teenage victims as well,[1] and most had been convicted of more than one crime. Among rapists, 12 percent had been convicted of more than one rape or attempted rape, 39 percent also had convictions for burglary or robbery, 29 percent for abduction, 25 percent for sodomy, and 11 percent for first- or second-degree murder. Since most of the prisons used in this project were maximum-security facilities, which primarily house violent and repeat offenders, it is no surprise that 85 percent of rapists had previous criminal histories; however, only 23 percent had records of previous sex offenses. Their sentences for rape and accompanying crimes ranged from 10 years to 7 life sentences plus 380 years. Most of the men had sentences of 10 to 30 years, but 22 percent were serving at least one life sentence. The vast majority were young, between the ages of 18 and 35 years, when they were interviewed; 46 percent were white, and 54 percent were black. The majority of the rapists, 61 percent, had been raised as Baptists, undoubtedly due to the southern location of the prisons, but only 27 percent were practicing Baptists at the time of their interviews. Nonetheless, 59 percent of the men professed some form of current religious affiliation, while 41 percent expressed none. A total of 46 percent of the rapists were either married or cohabiting with a woman at the time of the rape, and only 26 percent had any history of emotional problems.

The typical rapist, like his father, was poorly educated when he came to prison, with only 20 percent having had a high school education or better; the majority, 85 percent, came from working-class backgrounds. Nonetheless, the majority of rapists reported steady employment prior to prison, although a sizable minority, 40 percent, were frequently unemployed. This pattern, low educational attainment and working-class background, must be interpreted with caution. It does not demonstrate that there are class differences in the propensity to rape, but it does suggest that there are class differences in the distribution of justice and the availability of legal resources in this society. Men at the low end of the class scale are less able to afford sophisticated defense attorneys who specialize in beating rape charges.

A sketch of the control group, consisting of other felons, is very similar to that of rapists. The majority of the men had multiple convictions for a variety of violent crimes, but primarily armed robbery (43 percent), first-degree murder (35 percent), breaking and entering (20 percent), malicious wounding (11 percent), and second-degree murder (8 percent). Like rapists, the majority of controls, 89 percent, had a history of past criminal acts.[2] The largest proportion of other felons were serving sentences of 11 to 30 years, but 20 percent had at least one life term to serve. Of the controls, 51 percent were black, and 49 percent white. Some 84 percent were between the ages of 18 and 35 years, and, like rapists, the majority had minimal educations before coming to prison and were from working-class backgrounds. A total of 68 percent of controls were either married or cohabiting at the time of their convictions, and 28 percent had histories of emotional problems. Indeed, these brief sketches reveal that the two groups of men, rapists and other felons, were well matched on general background characteristics but that the sample is biased in that it is not representative of higher-status males who commit crimes but are able to avoid prison.

Childhood and Parental Relationships

There is a widely held belief that early childhood experiences, especially those that occur within the context of the family, have primacy over all other or later influences and are the most important determinant of future behavior. With respect to rape specifically, some have asserted that boys who grow up in female-headed or female-dominated households become "hypermasculine." The argument is that such boys attempt to overcompensate for their female identification and demonstrate or prove their masculinity through aggressive acts often targeted at women.[3] For example, a study of delinquents in an Ohio school for boys concluded that boys from mother-based households (1) had exaggerated perceptions of their manliness and toughness, (2) placed great emphasis on tough behavior, (3) emphasized sexual athleticism and the idea of women as conquest objects, (4) were more impulsive and hostile, and (5) were overly predisposed to peer pressure and to engage in excitement-oriented, high-risk behavior (Silverman and Dinitz 1974). Thus, the researchers conclude that because of their experiences in mother-headed families, these boys come to regard antisocial and aggressive behavior as a means to maintain the image of "real man." I am not disputing that the boys in this study, as well as some men, display "hypermasculine" characteristics. But it is important to examine the causal assumption that underlies the theory—that experience in mother-headed families is the origin of "hypermasculinity." The problem with these theories is that they dwell on the "unfitness" of mothers to raise their sons, rather than on sexually violent men. In the final analysis, mothers are blamed, at least indirectly, for their sons' violence toward women.

The composition of childhood household did not distinguish rapists from other felons in this study. In the case of both groups, a little less than half grew up with both of their natural parents and the remainder of both groups lived with their mothers or, to a lesser degree, a guardian, or in a juvenile home. In light of the similarity between rapists and other felons, the female-headed/dominated household explanation contributes little to an understanding of sexually violent men specifically.

The literature that blames mothers for their sons' sexual aggression accuses mothers of many vices, but, particularly, as one prominent psychiatrist describes it, of being "seductive but rejecting" (Abrahamsen 1960, 163). In this view, rape is an act of hostility toward a mother figure, an attempt to force her into submission. If there is any validity to this explanation, rapists should report dissatisfaction with their childhood relationships with their mothers, and they should express negative feelings toward their mothers.

Contrary to the rejecting mother theory, it was fathers with whom rapists, and to a slightly lesser degree other felons, had problems. Among rapists, 51 percent had been abandoned by their fathers by the age of 18 years. When asked which family member they were closest to, 41 percent of rapists answered mother, but only 13 percent said father. Similarly, when asked for the family member to whom they had been least close, 38 percent of rapists responded father, while only 8 percent indicated mother. Siblings accounted for most of the remainder of both responses. Additionally, when asked to describe their relationships with their mothers, 83 percent of rapists responded close or very close, while a similar description was given for fathers by only 44 percent of these men.

The treatment of female-headed/dominated households and blaming of mothers in the rape literature is another example of how androcentric bias has distorted perceptions of the roots and causes of sexual violence in this society. If experiences in mother-headed/dominated families were the causal factor that best explained hostile, abusive treatment of women, we should expect to find sexual violence as a prominent feature of matrifocal societies, where family and kinship are organized around women and where men are peripheral to mother-daughter-sister-aunt groups who live, work, and raise their children together in the same female-dominated households for life.[4] In fact, the opposite is true. Matrifocal societies tend to be peaceful, stable, and noncompetitive, and warfare and the denigration of women are rare. By contrast, it is in male-dominated patriarchal societies, where women have little or no social, political, or economic power in or out of the family, that rape and other types of female abuse are found (O'Kelly and Carney 1986). All of this suggests that it is not mother-headed households that are the problem but rather the societal context in which these family units exist. Furthermore, if parental relationships are related to adult sexual violence in patriarchal societies, the findings in this research strongly suggest that it is fathers, not mothers, who are primarily culpable. The lack of cultural expectations regarding the role of father has led us to ignore the effects that absent or distant fathers have on their sons' social and psychological development. Absent fathers also contribute to the alarming level of poverty among women and their children, which is the source of many of the problems these households experience.

Family Violence and Child Abuse

Explanations related to family violence, child abuse, and particularly childhood sexual abuse are currently in vogue and enjoy widespread acceptance as one of the main causes of men's sexual violence. Because of strongly held beliefs in the causal connection between these childhood experiences and rape, the men were carefully probed to determine the extent to which they had been victimized by such acts as children. It is important to point out, as Chapter 4 will demonstrate, that many of the rapists used excuses to explain their sexually violent behavior. The fact that childhood family violence and sexual abuse have become socially acceptable excuses for adult antisocial behavior suggests that it would be in the interest of these men to exaggerate, rather than minimize, the amount of victimization they had experienced in their childhoods.

It was true that family life was turbulent for many of the rapists. Almost half of the men felt that their childhoods could be characterized by instability, no doubt linked to their fathers' abandonment and consequent family poverty, and the fact that almost half had spent at least a portion of their childhoods living outside the family group in detention centers and foster homes. A number of the rapists had also witnessed violence in their families during childhood. Half of the men reported seeing their fathers hit their mothers, and one-third indicated that these incidents resulted in physical injury. The other felons group experienced somewhat less violence, with 36 percent reporting hitting and 14 percent noting injury.

Child abuse was reported less frequently than other forms of violence in the family. A total of 34 percent of the rapists and 32 percent of the other felons reported they had been victims of beatings that resulted in physical injury. Finally, 9 percent of rapists and 7 percent of the other felons confided they had been sexually abused as children. Thus, among rapists, 50 percent reported growing up in nonviolent families, 66 percent stated they had not been physically abused as children, and 91 percent denied experiencing childhood sexual abuse.

I want to stress here that it is not my intention to diminish the seriousness of the violence that takes place within families, or the horrors of living, whether child or adult, in an abusive environment. There is no question that the family is a violent institution, but how could we expect otherwise when it functions within a society that seems to nourish a higher level of interpersonal violence than any other in the world. Indeed, there is greater societal tolerance for violence directed at family members than for violence directed at strangers. That is, in most jurisdictions, murder, rape, assault, or molestation of a stranger is punished more severely than spousal murder, wife beating, and rape or incest. But the task in this book is to understand rape and, here specifically, whether or not childhood and family experiences are the causal factors that best explain adult male sexual violence.

One approach to answering the question is to note that the majority of the rapists in this study did not experience family violence, child abuse, or sexual victimization, and consequently these factors cannot be used to explain their adult sexual violence. Additionally, if estimates of family violence and child abuse are accurate, it is apparent that some, if not most, boys who have these experiences do not engage in sexual violence as adults. Furthermore, girls as well as boys grow up in violent families and are physically abused as children, but the frequency of violent crime among women pales in comparison to the frequency among men. Similarly, even when considering possible gender differences in the reporting of child sexual abuse, no study has determined that a larger proportion of boys than girls are sexually abused in childhood. Instead, estimated and reported ratios range from 11 to 48 boy victims per 100 girl victims (Finkelhor 1985). If sexual abuse in childhood causes adult behaviors such as incest, child molestation, and sexual violence, why is it that men, rather than women, commit the vast majority of these crimes? And why do men victimize primarily girls and women, when, for the most part, their own victimization was inflicted by men? For that matter, why don't the legions of girls and women who have been molested, raped, and otherwise brutalized by men respond through acts of sexual violence against their tormentors?

The problem with explanations that posit a direct causal relationship between childhood experiences and adult behavior is that they tell us nothing about the complex process by which behavior is actualized. These explanations cannot account for why girls who are sexually abused or who grow up in violent families do not engage in sexual violence as adults because they fail to consider the importance of structurally supported gender differences in cultural learning and social expectations that are a product of patriarchal societies. Why then do these simplistic explanations persist? This can be answered in a number of ways, and it is a question I will return to throughout this book. Let it suffice here to say that this narrow view of rape causation supports socially comfortable preventive policies aimed at remediating symptoms while remaining closed to the larger societal implications, which also are much more threatening to male privilege and the status quo.

Sexual Experiences and Relationships with Women

The nonfeminist rape literature, particularly the psychoanalytic literature, has traditionally emphasized the sexual aspect of rape.[5] The argument has been that rapists are sexually disordered, inherently different from other categories of men, and that many are "sexual psychopaths." (For a definition and discussion of sexual psychopathy, see Chapter 2.) The idea that sexual deprivation or frustration causes rape also appears in this literature. In this view, men who are deprived of sufficient consensual sexual opportunities become frustrated and rape to satisfy their unfulfilled sexual desires. Note that this line of reasoning fails to consider why deprived men should rape, rather than seek other outlets, to relieve their sexual frustrations,[6] and it does not explain why

70

sexually frustrated women do not commit acts of violence to relieve their condition. Because of the emphasis on sex in the psychiatric literature, a detailed sexual history was recorded for each of the men.

Contrary to the sexual deprivation/frustration thesis, the adolescent sexual experiences of the rapists in this study were unremarkable and similar to those of other felons. The typical rapist was 14 years old, compared to 13 years old for other felons, when he had his first sexual experience, and his usual partner was a female agemate. As previously noted, the majority of rapists were not sexually abused as children and, additionally, only a small proportion, 22 percent, remember being punished for childhood sexual behavior such as masturbation or "playing doctor." During adolescence, rapists did not appear to suffer from peer pressure to increase their sexual activity, as some have hypothesized. A total of 42 percent of rapists believed their sexual activity was about the same as that of their peers, 32 percent felt they had been more prolific than peers, and only 16 percent reported they felt they had had less sexual experience than their adolescent friends. Like most boys, the typical rapist learned about sex from his friends.

The amount of adult sexual activity among rapists was considerable, varied, and, again, similar to that of other felons. For instance, 89 percent of rapists, compared to 91 percent of other felons, estimated that before entering prison they had engaged in consensual sex at least twice a week; 42 percent of rapists, compared to 37 percent of the control group, indicated that they had consensual sex on a daily basis. While this level of sexual activity may seem high, considering the relative youth of these men when they came to prison it does not appear unusual. In addition, almost half of both the rapists and other felons claimed that they had engaged in group sexual activities involving two or more women, and 43 percent of both groups admitted to participating in at least one encounter where two or more males had sex with one female. While almost all of the men, 93 percent, insisted that in their view, the women had been willing or "known to enjoy such activity," the "enjoyment" of these women is suspect, since many of the rapists used similar justifications to explain their (other) sexually violent behavior (see Chapter 4). Not unlike young men generally, both rapists and other felons stated they would have preferred more sex than they actually experienced before incarceration. Despite this claim, which might have been influenced by their current relatively sexually deprived situation, these data suggest little support for the sexual deprivation/frustration thesis, nor do they reveal any substantial difference in the level of sexual activity of rapists and other felons.

The claim that men rape because they lack consensual sexual opportunities is also inconsistent with the observation that almost half of the rapists, 46 percent, were either married or cohabiting at the time of their offenses. Of the 31 percent who were ever married, 54 percent had had a single marriage, while 33 percent had had two marriages. Some 49 percent of the rapists reported having lived with three or more women, not counting their wives, and 62 percent had fathered children. In general, as a group, these men can be characterized as having had frequent, often brief, relationships with women and ample sexual opportunity—a pattern not unlike that of others of their age cohort.

Rapists' perceptions of their relationships with significant women are revealing.[7] From the perspective of these men, little discord existed in their marriages or in their living arrangements. In fact, the majority of rapists used very positive terms to describe their relationships with significant women, and only 16 percent expressed any dissatisfaction with the sexual aspects of these relationships. Countering rapists' perceptions is the fact that the majority of the men abused their significant women: 55 percent of rapists and 68 percent of other felons acknowledged having hit their significant women at least once, and 20 percent of rapists and 31 percent of controls admitted inflicting physical injury. Based on the general tendency of these men to understate the amount of violence they had used in their rapes (see Chapter 1), it is reasonable to speculate that they also may have underreported the frequency and severity of their abuse of significant women. Thus, it appears that the majority of rapists and controls engaged in acts of interpersonal violence against significant women at least occasionally and, in many cases, on a routine basis, but did not consider this violence as constituting discord in their relationships.

Because of the emphasis on sexual dysfunction in the psychiatric literature,[8] rapists and controls were probed for self-reports of these problems and, again, the two groups were strikingly similar: 42 percent of rapists and 43 percent of controls admitted to having experienced some dysfunction, such as erection difficulty, especially when under the influence of alcohol or other drugs. Indeed, had these numbers been lower, it would have cast suspicion on the honesty of the men and their willingness to reveal personally embarrassing information.

An interesting allegation found in the older psychoanalytic literature is that rapists are actually homosexuals with an aversion to "normal" sexual relations with women. Thus, we looked for evidence of homosexual interest, making it clear that the questions did not relate to prison sexual behavior. One rapist and three of the other felons indicated a sexual preference for men, which prompts me to conclude that homosexuality, like rejecting mother, has been used as a convenient psychiatric scapegoat for the sexual violence of heterosexual men.[9]

Related to the issue of sexual preference, only one rapist and no controls expressed sexual interest in children. Thus, while rapists and pedophiles traditionally are classified in the same criminal and psychiatric category—that is, sex offender—they seem to have little in common beyond the generic label bestowed upon them. The discrepancy between the myth of homogeneity, apparent in much of the psychiatric literature, and the reality of heterogeneity has led to misguided research comparing rapists to pedophiles and other categories of sex offenders, when understanding men who rape requires understanding how they differ from men who do not rape the adult women they sexually prefer.[10]

Rapists and other felons were also queried about deviant nonviolent sexual behaviors and, again, the two groups were similar. Their activities included the following: voyeurism—rapists 32 percent, controls 28 percent; occasional sexual inhibition—rapists 27 percent, controls 30 percent; frottage—rapists 25 percent, controls 26 percent; obscene telephone calls—

rapists 17 percent, controls 13 percent; and prostitution and/or pimping—rapists 14 percent, controls 12 percent. Less than 10 percent of either group admitted to exhibitionism, cross dressing, or zoophilia. Lacking an estimate of the prevalence of these behaviors among men, particularly young men, generally, the significance of these data for rapists specifically cannot be interpreted. However, it is possible to conclude that rapists and other felons were similar and that rape is not typified by a career that progresses from minor nonviolent sexually deviant acts that eventually culminate in sexual violence.

In summary, these data on the sexual experiences of men who rape fail to support a number of assertions that proliferate in the sex offender literature. Men who rape are heterosexuals, and they are not frustrated by a lack of consensual sexual opportunity. They are as likely as other men to have significant relationships with women, although perhaps more likely to have abused these women, and they father children. Further, the sexual experiences of rapists are unremarkable and do not differ significantly from those of other felons. While a small percentage of rapists may fit the profile of a sexual psychopath, there is no evidence that such a disorder characterizes the majority of men who rape. Thus, both sexual frustration/deprivation and sexual psychopathy lack utility as general explanations for rape.

Psychiatric History and Alcohol/Drug Use

Perhaps the most frequent explanation for rape found in the psychiatric literature asserts that men who rape "suffer" from a form of mental illness that compels them to commit violent acts against women (for a full discussion of this perspective, see Chapter 2). The idea that rapists are "sick" also informs the public view of these men. This is in contrast to men who commit other types of violent crimes, such as armed robbery and even murder, whose behavior is rarely attributed to mental illness. Because of the overwhelming emphasis on mental illness in the literature, a detailed psychiatric history was recorded for each of the men.

Among rapists, 26 percent had received outpatient treatment for an emotional problem (not necessarily psychopathy),[11] and, of that number, 22 percent had been patients in psychiatric facilities. Some of this contact with the mental health system was a result of previous incarcerations. Indeed, a larger proportion of the control group, 28 percent, had received outpatient care, but slightly fewer, 20 percent, had received inpatient treatment. Only 9 percent of rapists had been in psychiatric facilities more than once, and a small number, 11 percent of those ever hospitalized, had spent in excess of six months in such facilities. The pattern was similar for other felons, except the number hospitalized more than once was smaller, 3 percent. Thus, the majority of rapists did not have histories of psychiatric involvement or mental illness, nor were their histories markedly different from those of other felons. Similarly, in several studies of sexually aggressive college men, researchers have failed to find support for the psychopathological model (Briere and Malamuth 1983; Koss et al. 1985). And Smithyman (1978, 49) concludes, from his research on "undetected" rapists:

The rapist must solve all the problems of daily living like everyone else. In the case of the men participating in this investigation, they apparently do so to a degree somewhat better than expected. . . . Along almost every dimension examined, these men seemed not to differ markedly from the majority of males in our culture. Indeed, there appears to be such a wide variety of backgrounds among males who rape that no sweeping generalizations about them should be made.

Attempted suicide, another indicator of mental health status, did distinguish rapists from other felons: 31 percent of rapists, compared to 19 percent of other felons, had attempted suicide at least once. Several points are relevant to understanding these somewhat surprising data. First, the vast majority of suicide attempts by rapists were made by admitters rather than by deniers. Additionally, while the majority of attempts made by other felons occurred prior to their crimes, among rapists suicide attempts were equally

75

distributed between before and after first rape. Specifically, it was white admitters who had incorporated the image of rapist into their self-concepts who were the most suicide prone.

Rapists, 40 percent, were somewhat more likely than other felons, 31 percent, to have used alcohol on a regular or heavy basis prior to incarceration. Additionally, compared to 23 percent of other felons, 44 percent of rapists said they were serious drinkers before the age of 15. The typical rapist also smoked marijuana, at least occasionally, but only 28 percent indicated sustained heavy use of stronger drugs. It should be pointed out that these data were gathered between 1980 and 1982, before the proliferation of cocaine and crack in the United States, and, as a group, these rapists were not heavily involved in drugs. While the link between drug use and theft or robbery is clear (users commit crimes to support their habits), it is apparent that something more fundamental is involved in rape. For this group of rapists, sexual violence occurred primarily in the absence of drugs. However, a discussion of the role alcohol and/or drugs did play in their rapes will be presented in Chapter 4.

To summarize, these data do not support the widespread belief that most men rape because they are "sick," nor do they reveal that rapists, as a group, are more likely than other felons to be mentally ill. More precisely, convicted rapists were no more likely than other felons to have come into contact with the mental health system. Although both groups may have had greater involvement than a random sample of their peers, part of this is due to the nature of a prison sample and the fact that their criminal behavior puts them in contact with the mental health system. The rate of attempted suicide among rapists was higher than among other felons. However, in light of the fact that rapists' attempts were evenly divided between pre- and postrape, in contrast to other felons, where the majority of attempts were preoffense, they are as much an indication of rapists' negative evaluation of their behavior as they are evidence of prior emotional disturbance. Finally, if evidence of a history of mental illness fails to emerge for the majority of men in an incarcerated sample of rapists, it is even less likely to be typical of men who rape but are able to avoid detection and/or prison, as demonstrated by the research on male college students (Briere and Malamuth 1983; Koss et al. 1985).

Careers in Crime

Earlier in this chapter, the current convictions of rapists and other felons were described. The object in this section is to examine the criminal careers of the two groups to determine whether anything in rapists' criminal backgrounds distinguishes them from other felons or could have been used to predict that they would rape.[12]

The majority of both rapists and other felons had an impressive history of arrests and involvement in criminal activity. For example, 52 percent of rapists and 39 percent of other felons had been arrested by the age of 15, and the majority of both groups—84 percent of rapists and 97 percent of other felons—had been arrested for at least one nonsexual offense prior to their current convictions. Some 44 percent of rapists and 50 percent of other felons had been arrested in excess of three times, and some of the men had been arrested so many times, they could only estimate the number. Thus, the majority of both groups had a history of criminal charges, and, for both groups, the majority of these charges were for property crimes (such as breaking and entering) or property-person crimes (such as armed robbery) rather than person-only crimes (such as rape or murder).

The typical rapist did not have a history of arrests for rape. Indeed, only 25 percent of rapists had been arrested for a sex offense prior to their current convictions and prison sentences had resulted for only 12 percent of this group. Thus, the typical rapist had not previously been incarcerated for rape. In fact, only 37 percent of rapists, compared to 68 percent of other felons, had been in prison for any reason prior to their current sentences.[13]

The typical rapist had been convicted of one rape, although a small number, 13 percent, had multiple rape convictions. Nonetheless, some of the men with one rape conviction volunteered information about other rapes they had committed that had eluded detection or prosecution. Indeed, a few of the men appeared to have committed so many rapes that they experienced difficulty in separating the details of each. Invariably, regardless of the rape a man had been convicted of, the rape he preferred to talk about was the one that involved the least amount of physical violence and that did his self-image the least amount of damage.

The question addressed in this section was, in contrast to the criminal histories of the other felons, whether anything in the recorded criminal backgrounds of rapists could have been used to predict that they would rape. The answer, for the majority of the men, is no.

Attitudes and Beliefs

If rapists are not very different from other felons when family, sexual, psychological, and criminal histories are compared, is there anything that distinguishes men who rape from men who do not? This section will explore the possibility that the difference has to do with attitudes and beliefs related to rape. It is important to understand that the socialization of all members of a society is influenced, to some degree, by a common set of values. Thus, men who rape should not harbor beliefs that are drastically different from those of other men, but they may have more extreme attitudes. The difference should be one of degree, not of kind.[14]

Women on a Pedestal

Simple logic suggests that men's attitudes toward women should be related to rape. To explore this connection, Spence et al.'s (1973) short version of the Attitudes Toward Women Scale (AWS) was used to compare rapists' and other felons' preferences for traditional versus liberal or feminist gender role attitudes and behavior.[15]

Contrary to the expectation that rapists would be characterized by very traditional gender role attitudes, their mean score of 68.4 (out of a possible 100) on AWS suggests that, at least at the time of their interviews, rapists were more liberal than traditional. Additionally, there was no significant difference between the attitudes of rapists and other felons or between black and white offenders. Furthermore, contrary to the hypothesis that, consistent with their failure to view their behavior as rape, deniers would express more traditional attitudes toward women than admitters, no significant difference between these two groups was found.

These rather surprising findings require some elaboration. The widely used AWS was developed in the early 1970s and may be more appropriate to the period in the United States before progress had been made in expanding the rights and roles of women. A belief in the ideal (still unrealized) of equality in education and pay is less radical now than when the scale was developed. Nonetheless, I had trouble comprehending the apparent liberalness of these rapists. To discover how they would compare to a contemporary nonincarcerated population, a sample of college students from a large university in the same state was administered the AWS.[16] The addition of college students produced some expected differences. Women were more feminist than men, while a comparison by race revealed no significant difference. Additionally, college students, both men and women, were significantly more feminist in their attitudes toward women than were the offenders.

The experience of interviewing the rapists had given the distinct impression that they were more liberal on some aspects of the female role than on others. To test this perception, the scale was reconstructed by extracting questions that express three dimensions of attitudes. The first dimension consists of questions that express equality for women in occupation, pay, and education. The second dimension represents equality in the domestic sphere, such as equal rights to family property and income and the idea that men should share responsibility for housework and child care (keep in mind, these are ideals). The third dimension consists of attitudes labeled "women on a pedestal," which represent the idea that women need male protection and that they should be more virtuous than men, for example, by not telling dirty jokes, getting drunk, or paying their share of the cost of a date.

As expected, major differences did occur in the degree of adherence to the values represented by each dimension.[17]

That is, rapists and other felons, and admitters and deniers, were most liberal on the occupation dimension, somewhat less liberal on the domestic dimension, and relatively traditional on the pedestal dimension. The same was also true for both men and women college students. Furthermore, for all groups the occupation and domestic dimensions were highly related to each other, meaning that if one were liberal regarding women's rights in the workplace, one would also be liberal regarding women's rights at home. Significantly, however, the pedestal dimension was not related to either of the other two dimensions, an indication that a different set of values was being expressed in the pedestal attitudes.

Another consideration important in interpreting the relatively liberal attitudes expressed by these men toward certain aspects of the female role is the fact that the data reflect the men's attitudes several years after the commission of their crimes. When asked if their attitudes had changed while they had been in prison, 44 percent of rapists and 30 percent of controls stated they believed they were now more liberal toward women than before, and they attributed the change to greater maturity and to the opportunity for reading and self-reflection that they claimed to lack on the outside. Pertinent to this observation is the sample bias—that is, better educated men, especially those attending school in prison, were more likely to volunteer for the research than were their less educated counterparts. At the time of their interviews, 49 percent of both rapists and other felons were attending school. Additionally, 34 percent of the rapists and 44 percent of other felons had achieved some college credits since incarceration, while only 7 percent of rapists and 13 percent of other felons had been to college prior to prison.

In order to determine whether education did, in fact, liberalize attitudes toward women, men who had received a GED (the equivalent of a high school diploma) or some college credits while in prison were compared to men who had not been engaged in educational pursuits. These results are quite interesting. While education clearly emerged as a positive factor for the rapists, it had no effect on the attitudes of other felons. For rapists, and particularly deniers, the more education they had, the more liberal were their attitudes toward women. Equally important, when AWS was broken into the three dimensions, education produced more liberal attitudes on the occupation and domestic dimensions but not on the pedestal attitudes. To determine if length of time in prison, rather than education, was changing attitudes, the men were divided into two groups, those who had served three or more years and those who had less time in prison. This comparison yielded no significant difference in attitudes.

These data suggest that pedestal values are fairly rigid, unchanged even by education. The implication is that values that give men more privilege than women and that promote a double standard by requiring women to be more virtuous than men may be important to understanding sexual violence. Perhaps, then, it is men with the most rigid demands for female virtue who are the best candidates for hostility because they cannot accept women as fully human, with the same rights of choice that men enjoy. These attitudes also allow men to believe that their victims were "legitimate victims" (for a discussion, see Weis and Borges, 1973) and that the victims "got what they deserved." Indeed, our culture supports such views of women (see Clark and Lewis 1977; LeGrand 1973; MacKinnon 1987), and this support is reflected in the excuses and justifications of rapists, as the following chapters will demonstrate.

Men Who Rape and Masculinity

In addition to understanding rapists' attitudes toward women, it is necessary to examine their perceptions of masculinity and the extent to which they conform to traditional male gender role expectations.

The gender role literature contains a number of theoretical attempts to identify attributes that are culturally defined as masculine. From their review of the literature on people's beliefs about the typical male, Cicone and Ruble (1978) suggest the qualities mentioned most often can be grouped into three areas: (1) how a man handles his life—emphasis on action and achievement orientation, including qualities like adventurousness, ambition, independence, courageousness, and competitiveness; (2) how a man handles others—emphasis on dominance, including traits like aggressiveness, powerfulness, and assertiveness; and (3) how a man handles his psyche—emphasis on levelheadedness, including qualities like logical, stable, unemotional, cool, and self-contained. Brannon (1976) suggests that masculinity consists of four themes: (1) "no sissy stuff"—avoidance of all things feminine; (2) "the big wheel"—acquisition of success and status, the breadwinner; (3) "the sturdy oak"—strength, confidence, and independence; and (4) "give 'em hell"—aggression, violence, and daring.

Combining elements of these two approaches, Doyle (1983) argues that five elements are central to the conception of the male gender role in the United States: (1) the antifeminine element—avoidance and dislike of anything connected to the feminine; (2) the success element—being a winner, a champ, *numero uno*; (3) the aggressive element—readiness to fight; (4) the sexual element—constant and insatiable desire for sex; and (5) the self-reliant element—being tough, confident, independent, determined, and cool. Pleck (1981), in contrast, distinguishes between traditional and modern versions of the male role. The traditional model validates masculinity through strength and aggression and discourages emotional sensitivity and feelings of vulnerability and weakness. Control over certain emotions, such as anger, is not expected. Men's most important friendships are with other men, but they are not expected to be emotionally intimate. Women are viewed as functional for sex and reproduction, and, unlike men, are expected to be virtuous and to defer to male authority—indeed, the pedestal syndrome. In contrast, the modern model validates masculinity through economic achievement and power, which requires intelligence and control over emotions like anger. Relationships with women are characterized by intimacy, romance, and companionship and are more important than relationships with other men, which may consist of little more than drinking together and engaging in sports activities.

With varying degrees of success, a number of studies have attempted to demonstrate that overidentification with the traditional model of masculinity, variously referred to as "hypermasculinity" or "compulsive masculinity," simply too much masculinity, is related to delinquent, violent, and sexually aggressive behavior. While not suggesting that "too much masculinity" is the sole cause of rape, combined with other attitudes, these values may indeed contribute to sexual violence.

Earlier in this chapter, theories that relate compulsive masculinity to maternal relationship or to growing up in a female-headed household were criticized because they ignore the role of fathers and the importance of cultural learning in favor of blaming women for all undesirable male attitudes and behavior. Rather than seeking psychodynamic origins and blaming mother, compulsive masculinity can be viewed as a form of normal deviance that is acquired through socialization in a culture that places tremendous importance on masculinity and male traits. Indeed, Fine (1986) demonstrates how Little League baseball, for example, teaches boys how to behave "properly": to display appropriate emotions—to be tough and intimidating; to control emotions, particularly fear and crying; to desire to win, by "hustling" even when injured; to maintain social unity among male peers; and, perhaps most important, to differentiate themselves from those who are female, weaker, and younger.

To get an indication of rapists' conformity to traditional aspects of the male role, each of the men was given the Compulsive Masculinity Scale (Silverman 1970).[18] This scale, with a range of 20 low to 40 high masculinity, measures four dimensions of the traditional male role: (1) toughness, fearlessness, and fighting; (2) preoccupation with developing an athletic physique; (3) sexual athleticism and the concept of women as conquest objects; and (4) defiance of authority. As expected, with an average score of 29.4 rapists were somewhat more compulsively masculine than other felons, whose average score was 28.3. There were no significant differences between blacks and whites or between admitters and deniers. And perhaps because survival in prison requires toughness, unlike the changes in attitudes toward women, neither education nor time in prison reduced compulsive masculinity.

Hostility toward women is another element in the traditional male role. To determine the extent to which rapists harbored hostile feelings toward women, each of the men was given the Hostility Toward Women Scale, which consists of three dimensions—distrust, dislike, and threat—with a range of possible scores from 20 low to 60 high hostility.[19] Like attitudes toward women, the findings were unexpected and contrary to prediction. Comparing rapists and other felons as well as admitters and deniers produced no significant difference in hostility, with all groups scoring around a low average of 33. There was, however, a small but significant racial difference, with blacks in the total sample somewhat more hostile toward women then whites in the total sample, and, once again, education, but not time in prison, was associated with lower hostility for rapists but not for other felons. A possible interpretation of these counterintuitive findings may have to do with the impact of rapists' immediate situation. That is, the experience of living in a female-deprived environment may have changed the value they placed on women and affected their feelings of hostility.

As expected, attitudes toward women were related to hostility toward women for all of the men. That is, the more traditional their attitudes toward women, the more hostile they were. This was especially true for rapists, where the relationship was stronger than for other felons. Additionally, the relationship was stronger for deniers than for admitters, a finding probably related to the formers' belief that they were in prison because of women and for behavior they did not define as rape.

Acceptance of interpersonal violence is yet another element in the traditional male role. Because of the violent nature of rape and the fact that research indicates that more force is often used than is necessary to gain victim compliance, each of the men was given the Acceptance of Interpersonal Violence Scale developed by Burt (1980). This scale measures the degree to which men feel that force and coercion are legitimate ways to gain compliance and, specifically, that they are legitimate in intimate and sexual relationships. Perhaps not surprising in a population convicted of violent crimes, all of the men expressed fairly violent attitudes. However, with possible scores ranging between 10 low to 40 high, rapists averaged 24.2 and other felons 23.9, indicating little difference between the two groups. Admitters and deniers were also similar, and, again, education was related to less violent attitudes.

Averages do not adequately convey the violent content of these attitudes, which, like the pedestal dimension, is a measure of their feelings about appropriate behavior in interpersonal relationships with women. To illustrate this point, over three-fourths of both groups believed that a man should not give up when a woman says no to sex. Also, 46 percent of rapists and 40 percent of other felons believed that a man was justified in hitting his wife, and almost two-thirds of both groups felt that a wife should not move out of the house if her husband hit her. Equally disturbing is the attitude of 45 percent of the rapists and 40 percent of the controls that some women like to be hit because they believe it means men care for them. And, as demonstrated earlier, not only did these men believe it was appropriate to use violence on women in their personal relationships, but these beliefs were translated into action, as the majority of the men did abuse their significant women.

It was expected that men who had either traditional or hostile attitudes toward women would also condone a high degree of interpersonal violence in their relationships with women. Analysis revealed that this was true for all men, but, once again, the relationship was much stronger for the rapists.

Myths, Stereotypes, and Definitions of Rape

A mounting body of research on the way in which attributions are made in rape cases clearly indicates that legal definitions tell little about how people define the behavior and judge responsibility for it. A review of this literature reveals that two sets of factors, in particular, affect the way people judge rape cases. One set has to do with the characteristics of the rape situation. These situational factors that influence people's perceptions of rape include the amount of force used, whether or not a weapon was present, the relationship between victim and offender (stranger versus acquaintance, friend, lover, or wife), and, perhaps most important, the perceived virtue of the victim and whether her behavior just prior to the rape was traditional or nontraditional. For example, using a series of rape scenarios that incorporate these factors, Williams (1978) found in her study of Anglo, black, and Mexican American males and females that all groups were more likely to want to prosecute the assailant when he was a stranger and used a weapon, especially if the victim was injured—a scenario appropriately labeled "popular rape." All groups were least likely to want to prosecute when a weapon and injury were absent and the situation described the victim as being picked up in a bar or when the assailant and victim were husband and wife. And in his study of actual rape trials, LaFree (1989) found that in cases where the major defense issue centered on whether a sexual act had occurred or been attempted or on whether the victim consented, the victim's life-style and her gender role behavior were more important even than measures of physical evidence and seriousness of the offense in determining jurors' evaluations. LaFree states that any evidence of a victim's drinking, drug use, sexual activity outside of marriage, or prior acquaintance with the defendant led jurors to doubt the defendant's guilt.[20] Defense lawyers, of course, use these factors to influence juries.

In addition to situational variables, other factors that are important to attribution in rape are the characteristics of the observer. Consistently, research has found that males attribute more responsibility to victims than do females (Calhoun 1978; Calhoun et al. 1976; Kanekar and Kolsawalla 1977). Gender role attitudes of the observer are also related to evaluation of fault in rape. Generally, research has found that people with traditional attitudes are harsher on the victim and more lenient toward the assailant than are people with feminist attitudes (Acock and Ireland 1981; Krulewitz and Payne 1978; Williams 1979). Indeed, research demonstrates that there is considerable variation in the way that people define rape and attribute responsibility for it. This lack of agreement also provides insight into understanding how it was possible for some convicted rapists to deny that their behavior constituted rape. While not precluding the possibility that personality dynamics might affect the need for some men to deny their crime, it is also apparent that, particularly in the case of rape, social definitions contribute support for these disclaimers.

Interestingly, the literature contains no record of an attempt to establish convicted rapists' definition of rape.[21] To fill this void, each of the rapists was asked to respond, in his own words, to the question, "What is a rape?" Essentially, three types of definitions were offered: (1) no physical force is necessary—anything against a woman's will; (2) physical force is necessary—no mention of weapons or injury as a prerequisite; and (3) a weapon must be used or beating and injury must occur for a rape to have taken place.

Analysis revealed important differences in the definitions of rape given by admitters and deniers. For example, 44 percent of admitters but only 11 percent of deniers gave the no force definition. In contrast, 45 percent of deniers, compared to 10 percent of admitters, mentioned a weapon, beating, or injury in their definition of rape. Among deniers, it was not unusual to receive the following type of definition, "Rape is when a woman's life is in danger, without a doubt, or when she is beaten unconscious . . . she can always lock her legs." In contrast, the following is an admitter's definition, "To dominate someone to the extent you impose your will when they say 'no,' to take without consent, violently or otherwise, if the victim is scared into it." These differences in types of response are consistent with the excuses and justifications that admitters and deniers used to explain their own rapes, as subsequent chapters will demonstrate. It should also be noted that admitters may have had more traditional definitions of rape at the time of their crimes.

Stereotypes and myths regarding rape are found not only in rapists' definitions; they abound in the artifacts of our patriarchal culture. Jokes about rape that target the victim and misrepresent her experience are commonplace, as evidenced by the tired, but well-publicized remark, "I think if rape is inevitable, relax and enjoy it" (Millsaps 1988), made by Indiana University basketball coach Bob Knight in an interview with NBC correspondent Connie Chung. Indeed, anthropologists of future centuries may well wonder what created a society of women so seemingly pleased with sexual violence.

Mounting research provides evidence that belief in rape stereotypes is the most powerful predictor of sexual aggression in men and is also related to a number of other phenomena, including narrow definitions of rape, not guilty verdicts in mock rape trials, denial of injury to rape victims, and blaming victims for their own victimization (for a full discussion, see Chapter 2). In order to determine the extent to which convicted rapists believed common myths, a rape stereotype scale was developed for this project.[22] The scale incorporates four major dimensions of rape myth: (1) victim precipitation—the belief that characteristics or behaviors of women cause men to rape; (2) victim responsibility—the belief that women could avoid rape if they tried; (3) victim participation—the belief that women ask for and secretly enjoy rape; and (4) false accusation—the belief that women use the charge of rape vindictively to punish men.

Consistent with the rape stereotype research, belief in these common myths did discriminate rapists, with an average score of 29.0, from other felons, with an average score of 27.7, on the scale, which ranges from 12 low to 48 high belief in stereotypes. For example, among rapists, 69 percent agreed that most men accused of rape are really innocent, and 65 percent believed that women cause their own rapes by the way they act and the clothes they wear. When a woman accuses a man she knows of rape, 59 percent believed she changed her mind after voluntary sex; 54 percent believed women should be responsible for preventing their own rapes; and 46 percent favored changing laws to make it more difficult for women to prove they had been raped. Deniers were significantly more likely to believe these stereotypes than were admitters, as were blacks, as a group, when compared to whites, as a group. And, once again, education, but not length of time in prison, significantly diminished belief in these stereotypes for rapists and somewhat less for other felons.

As expected, belief in rape stereotypes was related to both hostility toward women and acceptance of interpersonal violence. That is, the more hostile the man's attitudes toward women and/or the more accepting he was of interpersonal violence, the stronger his belief in rape stereotypes. For admitters, but not deniers, belief in pedestal values was also related to rape stereotypes. This pattern suggests that for admitters, rape is associated with perceived "nonvirtuous" behavior of women, or of a particular woman, while for deniers, hostile feelings and a belief in the appropriateness of violence toward women are more the issue. This observation finds support in the data presented in subsequent chapters. Indeed, sexual violence is complex and cannot be reduced to a single simplistic cause.

A final note. This exploration of rapists' attitudes did not produce the dramatic results that one might have predicted. In part, the reason for this was methodological. Obviously, the best way to understand the relationship between attitudes and rape would be to use the impossible strategy of interviewing men shortly before they rape. The attitudes of the men in this study were measured at varying points in time after they committed their rapes, and, as the data on education suggest, the attitudes of some of the rapists had probably changed somewhat. The observation that uneducated men harbored more traditional attitudes than those men who were educated while in prison suggests that prison-educated rapists may have been less liberal in their views of women, masculinity, violence, and rape at the time of their crimes. Thus, we can tenuously infer that there was greater similarity in the attitudes of non-prison-educated men at the time of their rapes and the time of their interviews than was the case for education-exposed rapists—a clear message about the importance of education in prison.

Additionally, in comparing rapists and other felons, it is important to keep in mind that some proportion of the other felons group were undoubtedly sexually aggressive, if not rapists. This assumption is substantiated by the data on hidden sexual aggression among male college students (see Chapter 2), as well as by the prevalence of abuse of significant women reported by the other felons. Thus, if attitudes are related to behavior, the presence of aggressors in the control group would diminish differences between rapists and other felons.

Finally, failure to find relationships with more statistical significance is due, in part, to the procedures used. Results were always in the predicted direction, but other factors, such as the sizes of the numbers being compared, may have affected significance. Despite these problems, there is something to be gained from attempting to understand the attitudes and beliefs of men who rape. With this information a profile of the type of man in prison for rape can be constructed, and a cautious statement can be made about how he differs from other felons.

Summary Profile of Convicted Rapists

A significant minority of the rapists in this study grew up in unstable or violent homes. They had poor relationships with their fathers; some experienced child abuse, but very few had been sexually abused. The same was true for other felons. As adolescents and adults, rapists' sexual experiences were considerable, varied, and no different from those of other felons. For the most part, they were not sexually frustrated at the time of their rapes, nor did they lack consensual sexual opportunities. The incidence of reported homosexuality, sexual dysfunction, and nonviolent sexual deviance was no greater among rapists than among the other felons. Like other felons, rapists were capable of forming relationships with women, although, in the case of both groups, these relationships can be characterized by at least occasional abuse of significant women. Despite the popular belief that men who rape are "sick," the majority of rapists did not have histories of mental illness, and their contacts with the mental health system were no more extensive than those of other felons. More rapists than other felons reported having attempted suicide, but half of these attempts occurred after they had raped, and thus are not necessarily an indication of emotional problems that caused them to rape. The criminal careers of rapists and other felons were also very similar, with ample evidence of criminal activity prior to the current offense and, in many cases, dating back to adolescence. The majority of rapists did not have histories of arrests or convictions for sex offenses, and, like the other felons, the majority of their previous convictions were for crimes against property rather than against people.

Indeed, this background profile of convicted rapists does not suggest a unique category of criminal offender. Instead, it reveals a typical felon with no remarkable history to suggest a greater likelihood to rape. That is, the backgrounds of these rapists contain those factors known to be associated with non-white-collar crime generally, but provide little insight into rape specifically.

What can be concluded about the relevance of attitudes and beliefs to sexual violence? Rapists and other felons were similar in their attitudes toward women and their hostility toward women, and men who believed strongly in the double-standard pedestal values also harbored a degree of mistrust and dislike of women. This pattern was especially true for rapists, whose rigid, moralistic perspective on appropriate female behavior was consistent with very hostile attitudes toward women. Since all of the men were convicted felons, many with long histories of violent crime, it was not a surprise to find that they were all somewhat accepting of interpersonal violence, but those who were the most extreme were also the most hostile toward women. In turn, these violent and hostile attitudes were related to belief in rape stereotypes, which was also a factor that distinguished rapists from other felons.

This profile reveals a frightening and obviously dangerous group of men, but does it suggest that men who rape are "sick"? At the risk of repetition, it must be emphasized that the factors that distinguish rapists—belief in a double standard, belief in rape stereotypes, and strong identification with the traditional male role—find general support in our culture. While the data do not permit the claim that men who rape have a unique set of attitudes that sets them apart from other men, they do suggest that men who fit this profile are good candidates for sexual violence toward both significant women and anonymous women.

Notes

1 Offenders whose primary convictions were for incest, child rape or molestation, statutory rape, or sodomy of a male were not included in the study.
2 It should be pointed out, again, that while none of the men in the control group had a current or past conviction for rape, we cannot assume that none of them had ever committed a sexually violent act.
3 Talcott Parsons (1947) is responsible for introducing the concept of compulsive masculinity to describe men raised in female-headed households.
4 I am referring here to matrilineal, matrilocal societies, where kinship is traced through the female bloodline and daughters remain in the households of their mothers after marriage. In such societies, men divide their time between the households of their sisters and the households of their wives.
5 I argue that the exclusive emphasis on violence in the feminist literature and the exclusive emphasis on the sexual in the psychiatric literature both miss the mark. Rape is a violent act, but it is also a sexual act, and it is this fact that sets it apart from other crimes. See Chapter 5 for a full discussion of this issue.
6 I do argue in Chapter 5 that sexual access is one motivation for rape, but not due to sexual frustration, as the psychiatric literature suggests.
7 I was also interested in obtaining some measure of rapists' beliefs regarding women's experience of sex. In general, they demonstrated somewhat limited sexual knowledge. For example, when asked what type of sexual activities they thought turned women on, only 14 percent mentioned anything other than direct genital stimulation. In fact, many of the men greeted this question with a blank stare. Presumably, the answer was so obvious, they did not understand why they were being asked. The majority of rapists also believed that most women enjoy sex and that most women do not like to be "overpowered" or "hurt" during sex. This is consistent with the discussion in Chapter 5—that for some rapists, part of the pleasure of rape is knowing that women do not enjoy it. Finally, while I have no explanation for this finding, 69 percent of rapists believe that most women are not sexually satisfied by their husbands.
8 In the late 1970s, with the invention of a penile plethysmograph, an instrument that quantifies increases in penile

circumference as a measure of erection response, psychiatrists and psychopathologists began experimenting to determine the factors that contribute to rapists' sexual arousal and how their responses might differ from those of other men. For example, in a series of experiments, Gene Abel and his colleagues measured the erection response of rapists and controls while they listened to erotic heterosexual audiotapes, some depicting enjoyable, mutually consenting sex, and others depicting forcible sex with the infliction of pain. In general, they found that rapists were equally aroused by consenting and forcible depictions, while controls were aroused more by nonforcible scenarios. Much of their research was flawed, however, due to the choice of the control groups, premised on the assumption that the most appropriate comparisons are between types of sex offenders. Thus, the conclusion that rapists have deviant sexual arousals was based on comparisons with pedophiles, exhibitionists, voyeurs, and even gay males (during this period in psychiatric history consensual homosexuality was regarded as a form of sexual deviance) rather than on comparisons with other heterosexual men whose sexual preference is adult women. (Abel and his colleagues have published a number of penile studies; see, for example, Abel et al. 1975, 1977, 1978.)

Other psychiatrists and psychopathologists have also experimented with similar approaches (for a review of studies using this approach, see Knight et al. 1985). In one such study, the erection responses (measured as a percentage of full erection) of ten convicted rapists and ten male graduate students were recorded while the men listened to audiotape depictions of mutually consenting sex, rape, and nonsexual assault (Barbaree et al. 1979). Experimenters found that both rapists and graduate students experienced some measurable arousal to all three conditions, and, in both groups, the greatest arousal (a mean of 50 percent of full erection) was to mutually consenting sex. However, rapists' arousal to mutually consenting sex and to rape was almost equivalent, while graduate students experienced an average decrease to 35 percent of full erection in the rape condition. In the assault condition, the response of graduate students, an average 10 percent of full erection, was roughly half of rapists' average 22 percent of full erection. The experimenters suggest that it is not necessarily that force, violence, and nonconsent of the woman evoked sexual response in the rapists, but that force, violence, and nonconsent of the woman failed to inhibit their sexual arousal. It is also possible, as the experimenters note, that the graduate students were aware of the social pressure against arousal to rape cues and were able to exert voluntary control over their sexual arousal.

9 In one respect, however, the sexual preferences of these rapists may differ from those of other men. In contrast to the typical older male–younger female dating and mating pattern, when asked for the age of their preferred sexual partners, 43 percent of rapists, compared to 28 percent of other felons, indicated they were interested in women older than themselves. When those who responded "women of any age" are added, fully 65 percent of rapists, compared to 48 percent of controls, expressed sexual interest in women who were older than they were. These data are open to differing interpretations. However, before concluding that these rapists desired a "mother figure" in sexual relations, it is necessary to consider their relative youth and that older women did not necessarily mean women of their mothers' generation. In various parts of the interview, they voiced preferences for sexually experienced women, and they believed such women were likely to be older than they were.

10 For a discussion of sex offender classification, see Knight et al. (1985).

11 It is not possible to be more specific because most of the men did not know what their psychiatric diagnoses were.

12 As used here, the term *career* does not mean an economic activity from which the offender derived his livelihood, but rather the longitudinal process and pattern of criminal activity. Thus criminal careers can be studied in the same way as any other career.

13 The larger proportion of repeat offenders in the other felon group is partially explained by the practice in this state of incarcerating all convicted rapists in maximum-security prisons. Thus, rapists start out at the top-security facilities rather than working their way through the system with successive convictions.

14 In addition to the attitudes explored in this chapter, several other scales were used in the research. For an additional discussion, see Marolla and Scully (1986).

15 It should be noted that there are drawbacks to AWS, such as the failure to distinguish between attitudes toward women and those related to men in some questions where both are present. Additionally, it was necessary to revise some of the questions—carefully, so as not to change the meaning—to remove the obvious middle-class bias and to make the language more understandable to men with limited educations. So, for example, an item such as "Intoxication among women is worse than intoxication among men" was changed to "Being a drunken woman is worse than being a drunken man."

16 The sample consisted of 30 black males, 65 black females, 54 white males, and 102 white females.

17 To observe the amount of difference in adherence to the values expressed, the means of each dimension were compared and t-tests were computed to indicate whether the means were significantly different.

18 Because this scale was initially developed for use with juveniles, it was necessary to reword the questions slightly to make the themes and argot relevant to adult men.

19 The Hostility Toward Women Scale was developed for this project when a search of the literature failed to produce a usable instrument—an interesting observation in itself. While the scale was not tested on a large population, it does have face validity. For example, items measuring distrust include "A man should never tell a woman how he really feels about her." Items measuring dislike include "Most women are cold people," and those measuring threat include "There are some times when a husband or boyfriend should hit his wife or girlfriend just to remind her who is the man."

20 LaFree (1989) also found that in rape trials where the major defense issue was correct identification of the defendant or his diminished responsibility for the act, victim characteristics were not used to influence the jury (see also LaFree et al. 1985).

21 Joyce Williams's (1978, 1979) research using rape vignettes was replicated in this project. In general, there was agreement between Williams's nonprison sample and the rapists regarding the noncontroversial "popular" rape, which involved a stranger abducting a woman at gunpoint. However, unlike Williams's sample, rapists were considerably less likely to define as rape a rape between strangers in which the victim was not injured and a weapon was not mentioned. For a full discussion, see Marolla and Scully (1986).

22 In developing the scale for this project, elements from two existing instruments were used and expanded; see Burt (1978) and Feild (1978).

4

Nothing Is Rape: Justifying Sexual Violence

In this chapter and the next, sexually violent men talk about their crimes, themselves, and their victims. Rather than focusing on the individual motives of men who rape, the object here is to examine how sexually violent men construct reality and how social and cultural factors contribute to these constructions. Together, these two chapters will demonstrate that, regardless of how brutal their behavior, from the perspective of these men, almost no act is rape and no man a rapist. But first, a brief introduction to the concepts that are used to organize rapists' accounts.

Learning to Rape

Sociologists have long noted that people can, and do, commit acts that they know others define as conditionally wrong and, having done so, engage various techniques to disavow their deviance and present themselves as normal. Through the concept of "vocabulary of motive," Mills (1940) was among the first to shed light on this process of disavowal. The transition from deviant to normal is accomplished through linguistic devices through which an individual, having anticipated the negative consequences of an act, attempts to interpret or explain it in terms that are culturally appropriate and socially acceptable. These interpretations or explanations are acquired through socialization—the process

by which we learn to appreciate the meaning and consequences of acts as well as the language needed to explain
them in socially appropriate terms. Thus, explanations are
drawn from knowledge acquired through contact with one's
culture, and they reflect what individuals have learned to
expect that others will find acceptable.

"Accounts" is the concept developed by Scott and Lyman
(1968) to describe excuses and justifications, which further
elaborate the devices that people use to explain and remove
culpability when an untoward act has been committed (for
further elaboration of these techniques, see Hall and Hewitt
1970; Hewitt and Hall 1973; Hewitt and Stokes 1975; Stokes and
Hewitt 1976; Sykes and Matza 1957). In general, excuses admit
an act was bad or inappropriate but deny full responsibility
through appeals to accident or to biological or psychological
factors, or through scapegoating. In contrast, justifications
accept responsibility for an act but deny that it was wrong.
That is, justifications attempt to show how, in this situation,
the act was appropriate.

These chapters will demonstrate that admitters used excuses
in an attempt to explain why their behavior was rape but
they were not rapists. Deniers, in contrast, acknowledged
that rape is generally impermissible, but used justifications
to show how, in their situation, the behavior was appropriate
even if not quite right. Thus, an important part of learning to
rape includes the mastery of a vocabulary that can be used to
explain sexual violence against women in socially acceptable
terms. As men who have mastered this vocabulary, convicted
rapists have much to tell us about how sexual violence is made
possible in our rape-prone society.

More than an appropriate vocabulary of motive is involved
in learning to rape. The concept of role-taking is a useful tool
that can be used to explore further the perspective sexually
violent men take toward themselves and their victims. Two
forms of role-taking are particularly relevant to understanding
sexual violence. Reflexive role-taking, or the "looking-glass
self" (Cooley 1902), is the process of using the other person
to reflect expectations about and evaluations of oneself. A
related process, synesic role-taking, involves imaginatively
constructing the attitudes and feelings of the other person,

which provides the basis for anticipating their behavior (Lauer and Boardman 1971). Thus, it is through reflexive role-taking that a sexually violent man would see himself as his victim sees him and through synesic role-taking that he would imagine how his victim feels and predict her behavior. Role-taking is relevant to sexual violence because, theoretically, social control is mediated through an individual's awareness of self and other acquired in this process (Franks 1986).

Emotions are the expected outcome of role-taking (Shott 1979). Guilt, shame, and embarrassment are related to reflexive role-taking and are the result of seeing ourselves as others do. Empathy is related to synesic role-taking. Having placed ourselves in the position of the other person, we can feel their emotions or at least imagine what we would feel in a similar situation. Feeling sorry for someone, for example, is the result of synesic role-taking. For most people, role-taking emotions operate as powerful motivators of normative conduct because they encourage self-control, which is a major part of social control (Shott 1979).

Hochschild (1975), however, makes an important distinction between feelings and "feeling rules," the later being a form of social control that defines what we should feel, or the range of appropriate or desirable feelings, in various circumstances. She notes that culture impinges on feelings as well as feeling rules, and that both depend upon the situational context (Hochschild 1983). Thus, when self-control fails, it is because other factors have intervened and rendered the process inoperative.

These theoretical insights on vocabularies of motive and the interactions among role-taking, emotions, and feeling rules increase our ability to understand what renders social controls on sexual violence inoperative for some men in patriarchal societies. In this chapter the focus is on deniers, men who justify rape; in the next chapter, admitters, men who excuse rape, will be examined.

Denying Rape

Research discussed in Chapter 3 described a "popular," noncontroversial rape as one in which the assailant is a stranger and possesses a weapon, and, especially if the victim is injured, most people are willing to call it rape. On the other hand, when the victim violates traditional standards of gender role behavior by, for example, drinking, hitchhiking, or accepting a ride from someone met in a bar, some people, particularly men, are less likely to call subsequent sexual violence rape. Clearly, the key to justifying sexual violence to others is through accounts that make rape appear "controversial." We also saw that admitters and deniers were strong believers in rape stereotypes and that force and violence were integral to the definitions of rape given by deniers. The manner in which deniers define and judge responsibility for rape, in general, should have an effect on the way they interpret their own crime.

It is also possible that the rapes committed by deniers actually did contain more socially defined controversial elements than the rapes committed by admitters.[1] To explore this possibility, prison record presentence report descriptions of the two groups of crimes were compared.[2] In contrast to 72 percent of admitters, 66 percent of deniers were strangers to their victims. A weapon and/or injury was present in 74 percent of admitters' crimes, compared to 69 percent of deniers' crimes, and 11 percent of admitters, in contrast to 6 percent of deniers, murdered their victims. When the victim voluntarily accepted a ride while hitchhiking or in a bar, the rape was coded as controversial. This situation described 6 percent of admitters' crimes, compared to 22 percent of deniers' crimes.

Other differences that might affect men's willingness to define their behavior as rape were also examined. For instance, 43 percent of admitters, in contrast to 34 percent of deniers, were convicted of or admitted to more than one rape. Multiple convictions for a crime make justifying the behavior more difficult. Additionally, 23 percent of admitters, compared to 13 percent of deniers, had been convicted of a group rape, a situation relatively difficult to argue is normal and relatively easier to argue was someone else's fault.

Systematic discrepancies also appeared when admitters' and deniers' personal accounts of their crimes were compared to the official versions.[3] In general, admitters did not alter the facts of their cases, but they did understate the amount of physical force and violence they used to commit their crimes. Some deniers, however, did reconstruct events and change aspects of their crimes to make their guilt appear, at least, questionable. Of the 32 deniers' rapes, according to the records, 11 were between acquaintances, but 15 men claimed during the interviews to be acquainted with their victims. The official accounts described 7 rapes in which the victim had engaged in "controversial" behavior, but, according to deniers' accounts, this was true of 20 victims. Officially, weapons were present in 21 of the 32 rapes, but only 9 men acknowledged the presence of a weapon and only 2 of the 9 admitted it had been used to threaten the victim and gain compliance. Finally, in at least 7 of the rapes the victim had been seriously injured, but only 3 deniers admitted injury, and in 2 of those 3 cases, the victim had been murdered; in these cases the men denied the rape but not the murder. Finally, deniers never used words like *violent* or *rape*, choosing instead to emphasize the sexual component of their behavior.

This comparison reveals relatively minor, although predictable, differences in the two groups of crimes. While deniers' rapes were slightly more likely to contain elements that are socially defined as controversial, they also constructed their dialogue to ensure that "unpopular" accounts of their rapes were presented, accounts that they believed would cause others to question whether rape actually had taken place. In this respect, their familiarity with the cultural supports for rape was sophisticated, indeed.

To justify their behavior, deniers drew on the stereotypes of women in our rape-supportive culture to present their victims as both precipitating and to blame for the rapes. Though attempts to discredit the victims were more prominent in deniers' accounts, a few admitters likewise attempted to demonstrate that their victims were "legitimate" victims. Six

101

themes run through deniers' accounts, each constructed so that the victim and her behavior is presented in such a way that the man's behavior seemed situationally appropriate or justified—even if not quite right: (1) women as seductresses, (2) women mean yes when they say no, (3) women eventually "relax and enjoy it," (4) nice girls don't get raped, (5) guilty of a minor wrongdoing, and (6) macho man.

Women as Seductresses

Sexually violent men need not search far for cultural language that supports the premise that women are responsible for, or at least provoke, rape. In addition to common cultural stereotypes, the fields of psychiatry and criminology, particularly the subfield of victimology, have traditionally provided justifications for rape, often by portraying raped women as the victims of their own seduction. Through this ideological filter, criminal attacks are made to appear as if they were consensual sexual encounters. For example:

> Considering the amount of illicit intercourse, rape of women is very rare, indeed. Flirtation and provocative conduct, i.e., tacit (if not actual) consent, is generally the prelude to intercourse. (Hollander 1924,130)

Since women are expected to be coy about their sexual availability, refusal to comply with a man's sexual demands lacks meaning, and rape appears normal. The fact that violence and, often, a weapon are used to accomplish the rape is not considered. As an example, one psychiatrist has argued:

> The conscious or unconscious biological and psychological attraction between man and woman does not exist only on the part of the offender toward the woman but, also, on her part toward him, which in many instances may, to some extent, be the impetus for his sexual attack. Often a women [sic] unconsciously wishes to be taken by force—consider the theft of the bride in Peer Gynt. (Abrahamsen 1960, 161)

Like Peer Gynt, deniers attempted to demonstrate that their victims were willing and, in some cases, enthusiastic participants. In these accounts, the rape became more dependent upon the victim's behavior than upon the man's own actions.

An extreme view of the victim was presented by 31 percent of the deniers. Not only willing, she was the aggressor, a seductress who lured the man, unsuspecting, into sexual action. Typical was a denier convicted of his first rape and accompanying crimes of burglary, sodomy, and abduction. According to the records, he had broken into the victim's house and raped her at knife point. While he admitted to the breaking and entry, which he claimed was for altruistic purposes ("to pay for the prenatal care of a friend's girl-friend"), he also argued that when the victim discovered him, he had tried to leave but she had asked him to stay. Telling him she cheated on her husband, she had voluntarily removed her clothes and seduced him. She was, according to him, an exemplary sex partner who "enjoyed it very much and asked for oral sex."[4] "Can I have it now?" he reported her as saying. He claimed they had spent hours in bed, after which the victim had told him he was good looking and asked to see him again. "Who would believe I'd meet a fellow like this?" he claimed she said.

In addition to this extreme group, 25 percent of deniers said their victims were willing and had made some sexual advances. An additional 9 percent said the victims were willing to have sex for money or drugs. In two of these three cases, the victims had been either an acquaintance or picked up, which the rapists said led them to expect sex.

Women Mean Yes When They Say No

Despite these claims of victim willingness, it is significant that 34 percent of deniers described their victims as unwilling, at least initially, indicating either that the women had resisted or that they had said no. Despite this, and even though according to the records weapons had been present in 64 percent of these cases, deniers justified their behavior by arguing either that the victims had not resisted enough or that their no had really meant yes. For example, one denier was serving time for rape when he was convicted of attempting to rape a prison nurse. He insisted that the rape of the nurse had been completed, and said of his victim, "She semi-struggled but deep down inside I think she felt it was a fantasy come true." The nurse, according to him, had asked a question about his rape conviction, which he interpreted as teasing. "It was like she was saying 'rape me.' " Further, he claimed that she had helped him along with oral sex and "from her actions, she was enjoying it." In another case, a 34-year-old man convicted of abducting and raping a 15-year-old teenager at knife point as she walked on the beach claimed what he had done was not rape because he believed women like to be overpowered before sex, but to dominate after it begins.

> A man's body is like a Coke bottle, shake it up, put your thumb over the opening and feel the tension. When you take a woman out, woo her, then she says, "no, I'm a nice girl," you have to use force. All men do this. She said "no" but it was a societal "no," she wanted to be coaxed. All women say "no" when they mean "yes" but it's a societal "no" so they won't have to feel responsible later.

Claims that the victim didn't resist or, if she did, did not resist enough, were also used by 24 percent of admitters to explain why, during the incident, they thought the victim was willing and that what they were doing was not rape. According to these men, it was not until sometime after the crimes that they redefined their acts. For example, an admitter who used a bayonet to threaten his victim, an employee of the store he had been robbing, stated:

> At the time I didn't think it was rape. I just asked her nicely and she didn't resist. I never considered prison. I just felt like I had met a friend. It took about five years of reading and going to school to change my mind about whether it was rape. I became familiar with the subtlety of violence. But at the time, I believed that as long as I didn't hurt anyone it wasn't wrong. At the time,

I didn't think I would go to prison, I thought I would beat it.

Another typical case involved a gang rape in which the victim was abducted at knife point as she walked home about midnight. According to two of the rapists (both of whom were interviewed), at the time they had thought the victim had willingly accepted a ride from the third rapist (who was not interviewed). They claimed that the victim did not resist, and one of the men reported her as saying she would do anything if they would take her home. In this man's view, "She acted like she enjoyed it, but maybe she was just acting. She wasn't crying, she was engaging in it." He reported that she had been friendly to the man who abducted her, and, claiming not to have a home phone, she gave him her office number—a smart tactic which she used eventually to catch the three. In retrospect, this young man had decided, "She was scared and just relaxed and enjoyed it to avoid getting hurt." Note, however, that while he had redefined the act as rape, he continued to believe she enjoyed it.

Men who claimed to have been unaware that they were raping viewed sexual aggression as a man's prerogative at the time of the rape. Thus, they regarded their acts as little more than minor wrongdoing, even though most possessed or used weapons. Lack of resistance, despite weapons, became for them consent. As long as the victim survived without major physical injury, from their perspective, a rape had not taken place. Confiding that he used to believe women were "electrified by my touch," one young man explained that since he did not cause physical injury, he told himself it was what she wanted. Indeed, even U.S. courts have often taken the position that physical injury is a necessary ingredient for a rape conviction.

Women Eventually "Relax and Enjoy It"

It is clear that whatever else they may believe, sexually violent men believe the cultural stereotype that, once the rape began, their victims relaxed and enjoyed it. Indeed, 69 percent of deniers justified their behavior by claiming not only that their victims were willing but that they enjoyed themselves—in some cases, to an immense degree. Several men even boasted that they had made their victims' fantasies come true. Additionally, while the majority of admitters used adjectives such as "dirty," "humiliated," and "disgusted" to describe how they thought rape made women feel, 20 percent still believed that their victims, in particular, had enjoyed themselves. For example, one denier who, according to his records, had posed as a salesman to gain entry to the victim's house, claimed that the victim agreed to have sex with him for drugs. He bragged that the opportunity to have sex with him produced "a glow, because she was really into oral stuff and fascinated by the idea of sex with me. She felt satisfied, fulfilled, wanted me to stay, but I didn't want her."

In another case, a denier who had broken into his victim's house but who insisted the victim was his lover and let him in voluntarily, declared, "She felt good, kept kissing me and wanted me to stay the night. She felt proud after sex with me." Another denier, who hid in the victim's closet and later attacked her while she slept, argued that while she was scared at first, "once we got into it, she was okay." He continued to believe that what he did was not rape because "she enjoyed it and it was like she consented." Finally, more realism from a participant in a group rape and abduction who claimed the victim was a hired prostitute: he conceded that "by her movements she seemed to enjoy it, she seemed pleased, but it may have been because she was alive and going home."

Central to the usefulness of this justification was the denier's ability to produce a reason for the contradiction obviated by the fact that his victim had charged him with rape. Although 13 percent of men had no ready explanation, the majority suggested that their victims had not acted completely of their own volition in the matter. Primarily, two arguments were advanced: 28 percent claimed that someone else, such as a boyfriend, husband, or parent, had forced the victim to report or had done so themselves; an additional 28 percent maintained that the victim was forced to report rape as a cover-up for her own behavior or to avoid personal consequences. To further buttress these claims, 22 percent of deniers asserted that their victims had experienced a change of heart and admitted to culpability, and one man insisted that his victim had gone insane and been institutionalized as a result of her guilt over his conviction.

Contrary to the way that sexually violent men construct reality, the research is quite clear in showing that the extreme opposite is actually true. For example, one study found that not 1 out of 93 adult women rape victims gave a positive response to the question, "How did it feel sexually?" (Holmstrom and Burgess 1978a). In fact, a number of studies have shown that far from enjoyment, rape victims experience adverse psychological consequences, in some cases extreme, prompting some to move, change jobs, or drop out of school (see Burgess and Holmstrom 1974; Kilpatrick et al. 1979; Ruch et al. 1980; Shore 1979). Further, the trauma of rape is so severe that it disrupts sexual functioning, in terms of both frequency and satisfaction, for the overwhelming majority of women, at least during the period immediately following the rape and, in fewer cases, for an extended period of time (Burgess and Holmstrom 1979; Feldman-Sommers et al. 1979). Indeed, from the victim's perspective, rape is a life-altering experience that leaves an emotional residue that may never completely disappear. And even women who have not been victimized know that because they are women, they are rapable. This fear and the threat of rape causes many women to limit their activities in ways that men never have to consider. No, women do not enjoy sexual violence (for a discussion of women's experiences, see Stanko 1985).

Nice Girls Don't Get Raped

Perception of fault in rape is also affected by the belief that "nice girls don't get raped." Thus, any behavior on the part of the victim that is perceived as violating gender role expectations is perceived as contributing to the commission of the act. For example, in one study, hitchhike rape was defined as a victim-precipitated offense by male researchers (Nelson and Amir 1975). The victim's personal life also is used to discredit her and to present her as the legitimate object of sexual attack. Ultimately, a woman's sexual background can be used to deny her legal protection, as one criminologist makes clear when he states:

> The victim could be held unworthy of being protected by the law, either not being a female "of previous chaste character" or succumbing to false pretenses which would not deceive "a man of ordinary intelligence and caution." (von Hentig 1940, 307)

Echoing similar beliefs, it is significant that while they were not asked for the information, a large number of the men succeeded in interjecting something about the victim's sexual reputation into the interview. Once again, deniers, 69 percent, were more likely than admitters, 22 percent, to justify their sexual violence by claiming that the victim was known to be a prostitute, or a "loose" woman, or to have had a lot of affairs, or to have had a child out of wedlock, allegations they assumed would cast her in an unfavourable light.[5] For example, a denier who abducted his victim at knife point from the street stated:

> To be honest, we [his family] knew she was a damn whore and whether she screwed 1 or 50 guys didn't matter.

In another case, a denier who claimed to have known his victim by reputation stated:

> If you wanted drugs or a quick piece of ass, she would do it. In court she said she was a virgin, but I could tell during sex [rape] that she was very experienced.

When other types of discrediting biographical information were added to these sexual slurs, a total of 78 percent of the deniers used their victims' alleged reputations to substantiate their accounts. Most frequently, they referred to the victim's emotional state or alleged drug use. For example, one denier claimed his victim was known to be loose and, additionally, had turned state's evidence against her husband to put him in prison and save herself from a burglary conviction. Further, he asserted that she had met her current boyfriend, who was himself in and out of prison, in a drug rehabilitation center where they were both clients.

Evoking the stereotype that women provoke rape by the way they dress, a description of the victim as seductively attired appeared in the accounts of 22 percent of deniers and 17 percent of admitters, even though they were not asked for this information. Typically, these descriptions were used to substantiate their claims about their victims' reputations. Some men went to extremes to paint a tarnished picture of the victim, describing her as dressed in tight black clothes and without a bra; in one case, the victim was portrayed as sexually provocative in dress and carriage. Not only did she wear short skirts, but she was observed to "spread her legs while getting out of cars."

The intent of these discrediting statements is clear. The men were attempting to justify or excuse their own behavior by arguing that the women were "legitimate" victims who got what they deserved. In the men's view, a woman's lack of a pedestal gave them rights she was deprived of. For example, one denier stated that all of his victims had been prostitutes. Referring to them as "dirty sluts," he argued that anything he did to them was justified. The fact that the records showed they were not prostitutes is less the issue than his belief that prostitutes have no rights.

Such statements also reflect an effort to establish a reputational basis for claiming that the victim was guilty of false accusation and perjured herself in court. Not all of the men attempted to assassinate their victims' reputations with equal vengeance. Numerous times they would make subtle and offhand remarks like, "She was a waitress and you know how they are." Nevertheless, the intent was the same—to cast doubt on the victims' integrity or virtue and to make their own behavior appear more appropriate or reasonable. Their attempts to discredit and present a negative image of their victims take on greater meaning because, as the next section will demonstrate, they expended an equal effort to present themselves in what they thought was a favorable light.

Only a Minor Wrongdoing

It is interesting that, despite these justifications, the majority of deniers did not claim to be completely innocent, and they also accepted some accountability for their actions. Only 16 percent of deniers argued that they were totally free of blame. Instead, the majority of deniers pleaded guilty to a lesser charge. That is, they obfuscated or trivialized the rape by pleading guilty to a less serious, more acceptable charge. Thus, they accepted being oversexed, using poor judgment or trickery, even some violence, or being guilty of adultery or contributing to the delinquency of a minor, charges that are hardly the equivalent of rape.

Typical of this approach was a denier who met his victim in a bar when the bartender asked him if he would try to repair her stalled car. After unsuccessfully attempting the repair, he claimed the victim drank with him and later accepted a ride. Out riding, he pulled into a deserted area "to see how my luck would go." When the victim resisted his advances, he beat her. He explained:

> Then I did something stupid. I pulled a knife on her and I hit her as hard as I would hit a man. But I shouldn't be in prison for what I did. I shouldn't have all this time [sentence] for going to bed with a broad.

This man continued to believe that while the knife was wrong, his sexual behavior was appropriate.

In another case, the denier claimed he picked up his underage victim at a party and that she voluntarily went with him to a motel. According to the records, the victim had been abducted from a party at knife point. He explained:

> After I paid for a motel, she would have to have sex but I wouldn't use a weapon [his towering size and obvious strength meant he would not need a weapon to gain compliance]. I would have explained I spent money and if she still said no, I would have forced her. If it had happened that way, it would have been rape to some people but not to my way of thinking. I've done that

kind of thing before. I'm guilty of sex and contributing to the delinquency of a minor, but not rape.

Macho Man Image

In addition to the trivialization of their actions, a number of deniers also attempted to present themselves in a light that made it improbable that they would "need" to rape. For example, they used the argument that they had wives or girlfriends to demonstrate that there had been no reason for them to rape.

One-third of deniers expressed an extreme form of self-aggrandizement. Through their exaggerated pronouncements and extreme show of macho, these men seemed to capture the essence of what all deniers were claiming. The content of their bragging was primarily, though not exclusively, sexual and was an effort to emphasize information that augmented their view of self as nonrapists.

To demonstrate that they did not need to rape, it was not sufficient for these men to produce a single wife or girlfriend. Instead, they claimed to have an excessive amount of sexual opportunity. Typical of this bragging, one man claimed to have 20 women providing him with sex while he was in prison and even more while he was on the outside, and another argued that at his trial, five women had testified to the fact that he didn't need to rape. To substantiate claims of victim willingness, these men made extravagant statements about their attractiveness and desirability to women. The victim, in these cases, was presented as just one of many women who had sought the man's sexual favor. For example, one denier, reciting a list of women he claimed wanted divorces because of him, stated, "I don't think a woman has ever said no to me," and then confided his belief that he was in prison "because of my desirability, women are attracted to me."

To reinforce their contentions that their victims had enjoyed themselves, these men claimed to have superior sexual capacity and technique. For example, an older rapist stated with disdain, "Most men don't know how to satisfy a woman," and described his own sexual partners as "out

111

of their heads with enjoyment." It was not enough for these men to present themselves as just normal. Instead, they claimed to be multitalented superachievers, better at almost everything than anyone else. As one man put it, "I'm better at sex, sports, you name it—there just are too many things." And another denier, who believed "I'm better than the other guys in prison," claimed that he had retained "the best lawyer in the state" to free him. He vowed to get his victim to retract her charges, because "not only have I been cheated but the whole community is cheated because I'm in prison."

Finally, a few deniers even bragged about raping, though they did not view it as such. The message seemed to be that women found sex with them so rewarding that, despite recurrent acts of force, this was their first rape charge! Said one young man:

> If I thought a broad was dominant, I had to use strength. If she was passive, I'd still use strength, but not as much. Strength means pushing her on. I was a good actor—among the best! She would feel my palm on her head pushing her down if she played games. If I can show her the beauty of it, that's strength. Rape is force.

Imperceptiveness and Distorted Self-Image

Consistent with the justifications they used to explain rape, deniers distorted the image of sexually violent men. As a means of exploring the extent to which they were capable of seeing themselves as others do—reflexive role-taking—they were asked to describe how they thought their victims would have described them during and after the rape.

Not surprisingly, 45 percent of deniers gave no evidence of self-awareness, stating simply that they had no idea how their victims would have described them. However, another 45 percent responded to this question with positive answers, such as "good" "desirable," "gentle," and "friendly"—clearly the antithesis of the generalized image women have of men who rape. For example, a man who had abducted his victim as she walked down the street responded, "She told me I was a good lover and asked me where I had learned." Another denier, who had broken into his victim's house, commented:

> If she told the truth she would have described me like any other girl would. I try to make a girl enjoy herself as much as possible and she was no exception.

Only a scant 10 percent of deniers used terms like "cold," "nasty," or "psycho" to describe how they thought their victims had perceived them.

Since deniers either possessed a distorted self-image or had no self-awareness, predictably they also did not experience the emotions that mediate self-control—that is, guilt, shame, or embarrassment—as a result of their behavior. When asked to describe their feelings immediately after raping, the most frequent response, from 47 percent of deniers, was that they had no feelings at all; 26 percent said they felt scared or concerned for their own well-being, and a similar percentage described themselves as sexually satisfied. Indeed, from the perspective of these men, nothing much had happened. For example, one denier reported:

> I felt like I got what I wanted and had to get on with my business. She was of no more concern. I went to pick up my girlfriend.

Another denier summed it up for a number of the men: "I felt nothing. I got a piece of ass, no remorse."

"Just Something I Wanted to Do"

To investigate whether sexually violent men are capable of putting themselves in the position of their victim—synesic role-taking—they were asked to describe their victims' immediate reactions upon understanding that rape was imminent and also to explain how they thought their victims had felt during and immediately after the encounters.

Again, their descriptions of victims' initial reactions are consistent with the justifications they used to explain their sexually violent behavior, and reflect the common stereotype that women ask for and enjoy rape. Thus, deniers described their victims initially as willing or enthusiastic, or that they had been neutral or didn't seem to care, or that they had "said no but really meant yes." For example, one denier, who had abducted his victim as she walked on the beach, could have been recalling a pornographic novel when he claimed:

> She said, "No, I have my period. I'm a virgin." I laughed and rubbed her back and she accepted physically. Her legs spread and she thrust up to meet me. It was telepathic. This wasn't rape. I know what rape is.

Once the rape began, 36 percent of deniers ceased to notice their victims, and thus they said they didn't know or care how the victims had felt. However, 48 percent continued to claim that their victims had felt good or had enjoyed the "sex," while only 16 percent conceded that their victims had seemed scared or had disliked the "sex." However, when questioned about their victims' feelings following the rape, a larger number, 38 percent, responded with descriptions such as "bad," "relieved," or "angry." Still, 33 percent continued to say their victims had felt good or sexually satisfied, and the remainder either didn't know or didn't care.

Consistent with their lack of other emotions, deniers also did not experience empathy. When asked to describe their feelings for their victims during the rapes, a minority of the men claimed to have had good feelings, even love, for their victims, but the majority of deniers, 69 percent, reported feeling nothing or described their own physiological arousal. Additionally, it made no difference whether the victim was an acquaintance or a stranger. For example, a man who had raped his girlfriend's mother remarked:

> I don't think I had any feelings for her. At the time I think it was something I had wanted to do and was getting around to doing it.

Men who had raped strangers made similar comments, for example, "It was just to satisfy my needs. Let's face it, she was very tight, so I came quickly." At the time of their interviews, the majority of deniers continued to report no emotions or they expressed anger at their victims and a desire for revenge, or they were concerned for their own well-being. Speaking for a number of deniers, one man confided:

> I'm not sorry I did it, that's all. I'm not sorry for anything I ever did. I'm just not.

Justifying Rape

What, then, can be said about men who deny rape? Deniers' accounts reveal the essential elements involved in justifying sexual violence. Like others in our society, these men set very narrow limits for the behavior they would consider rape. Denying the existence of a victim, someone harmed by their behavior, they trivialized the seriousness of their offenses by pleading guilty to some minor wrongdoing. Additionally, they attempted to discredit and blame their victims, portraying them either as willing and eager or as deserving what they got, while presenting their own actions as situationally justified and themselves as lacking the need to rape. They are men who are deficient in role-taking, who lack self-awareness, and who can justify their actions because their construction of reality excludes women's perspectives. Thus, they are incapable of understanding the meaning of sexual violence to women.

Franks (1986) observes that in patriarchal societies, women are deprived of the power and status necessary to force men to role-take with them. In other words, power is inversely related to role-taking. People with greater power have less reason to take the role of others than do those in positions of less power. For the person with relatively less power, it is more important to be able to apprehend the attitudes and anticipate the behavior of the other (Thomas et al. 1972). The greater power of men in this society suggests they have less need to role-take, especially with women, than do women, especially with men, for whom role-taking is a survival strategy. Indeed, Franks notes that the invisibility of the female "self" from a male perspective is what enables men to omit women's perspective from the role-taking process involved in heterosexual conduct.

The abilities and capacities of individuals to role-take, as well as to experience emotions, are variable. Differences in symbolic universes or lack of shared meanings between people reduces role-taking accuracy (Lauer and Boardman 1971). Thus, disparity in the experiences and symbolic universes of women and men impose limitations on role-taking even in the best of situations. These gender differences also undoubtedly influence the feeling rules to which women and men respond in various situations.

Since patriarchal societies produce men whose frame of reference excludes women's perspectives, men are able to ignore sexual violence, especially since their culture provides them with such a convenient array of justifications. This also leads men who rape to ignore or misinterpret how they appear to their victims, who are to them only objects, and consequently their behavior produces none of the emotions expected to regulate their sexually violent acts. Indeed, it appears that this type of man rapes because his value system provides no compelling reason not to do so. In fact, none of the deniers thought of himself as a rapist. While this analysis is suited to deniers, the next chapter will demonstrate that the admitter is a quite different type of man who rapes.

Notes

1 As an indicator of the severity of the two groups' offenses, the current sentences being served by admitters and deniers were examined. What can be regarded as light sentences—20 years or less—were roughly the same for admitters, 23 percent, and deniers, 25 percent. The major differences appeared at the opposite extreme, with relatively more admitters, 33 percent, than deniers, 12 percent, serving a life sentence or longer. Since extremes affect averages, admitters averaged longer sentences, 51 to 60 years, compared to 31 to 40 years for

deniers. Men who not only raped but also murdered their victims were serving among the longest sentences and were primarily admitters. With men convicted of murder removed, since their sentences reflected the severity of both crimes, the average sentence for admitters dropped to 41 to 50 years, but still indicates slightly more severity in their sentencing than was the case for deniers.

2 Unfortunately, the completeness of information in the records was spotty, making it difficult, in some cases, to determine all relevant facts. For example, there might be no indication of the extent of the victim's injuries, making it necessary to surmise in other ways. If the record stated the victim had been shot, injury of some type had to have resulted. However, in cases where it was not possible to determine physical injury, the rape had to be coded as no injury.

3 As discussed in Chapter 1, prison records were used as a check on the validity of information contained in the records.

4 It is worth noting that a number of deniers specifically mentioned their victims' alleged interest in oral sex. Since their sexual histories revealed that the rapists themselves found oral sex marginally acceptable, the frequent mention is probably another attempt to discredit the victim. However, since a tape recorder could not be used for the interviews and the significance of these claims did not emerge until the data were being coded and analyzed, it is possible that this was mentioned even more frequently but not recorded.

5 I have always found this kind of logic particularly interesting. If it were used to justify other crimes it would mean, for example, that, having once given away money, a person would no longer be able ever to claim that he or she had been robbed.

5

No One Is a Rapist: Excusing Sexual Violence

Admitting Rape

The preceding chapter focused on the justifications used by men who deny rape to argue that, though their behavior may not have been completely proper, it also should not be considered rape. Such men were revealed to be lacking in self-awareness and in the capacity to understand sexual violence—a threat that, unlike women, they did not experience or fear. Admitters, men who acknowledge having raped, are the primary focus of this chapter and present a stark contrast to deniers. At the time of their interviews, admitters did regard their behavior as wrong and beyond justification. For the most part, they blamed themselves rather than their victims, although a small number of admitters reasoned that their victims had contributed to the crimes somewhat, for example, by not resisting enough, in their view. A few of these men also continued to express their belief that their victims had enjoyed the rape.

At the extreme, several admitters expressed the view that rape was worse than murder—an act of such moral outrage that it was beyond forgiving. Typical of those holding this sentiment is an admitter who exclaimed:

> I equate rape with someone throwing you up against a wall and tearing your liver and guts out of you. . . . Rape is worse than murder . . . and I'm disgusting.

Another young admitter, who frequently referred to himself as repulsive, confided:

> I'm in here for rape and in my own mind, it's the most disgusting crime, sickening. When people see me and know, I get sick.

Having acknowledged the moral reprehensibleness of their crimes, admitters used excuses to explain their behavior in a way that others would accept and that would do the least amount of damage to their self-image. Two of these excuses reflect popular beliefs about the causes of rape and appeal to forces outside of their control, which they said compelled them to rape. Through the use of excuses, they attempted to demonstrate either that intent was absent or that responsibility was diminished. Excuses also permitted them to view their behavior as idiosyncratic rather than typical and, thus, to believe they were not "really" rapists. Three themes run through these accounts: (1) alcohol and drugs, (2) emotional problems or the "sick" role, and (3) the nice guy image.

The Role of Alcohol and Drugs in Sexual Violence

The use of alcohol, and to a lesser degree drugs, is an explanation that both admitters and deniers used to account for their behavior. Indeed, alcohol and drugs appeared in the accounts of 77 percent of admitters and 84 percent of deniers, and both groups were equally likely to acknowledge having ingested primarily alcohol but in some cases also drugs prior to the rape—admitters, 77 percent, and deniers, 72 percent. They differed, however, in the way that alcohol and drugs were used in their accounts depending upon whether the intent was to excuse or to justify rape. Indeed, their social construction of the role these substances played in their rapes is a classic example of the self-interested use of a motive.

Other studies of sexual assault likewise have noted an association between alcohol consumption and rape (Groth 1979; Johnson et al. 1978; Queen's Bench Foundation 1976), although Coid (1986) points out that surprisingly little research actually has been done on the specific association between alcohol and sexual assault on women. For example, while Groth (1979) points out that among the rapists in his study, the amount of alcohol ingested was not a significant departure from customary habits, he also comments that while alcohol does not cause rape, in many cases it may be a necessary component in the process; in other cases, it may be a catalyst; and, in still other cases, it may be a parallel symptom of a disordered personality.

There is no question that alcohol produces chemical changes in the body that impair sensorimotor performance. What is increasingly questioned by researchers is the assumption that alcohol is also a moral incapacitator—a disinhibitor that changes behavior, usually for the worse. Despite widespread public belief about the way alcohol works, there is actually little empirical support for the disinhibition hypothesis; the idea that the chemical action of alcohol influences sexual and aggressive behavior. For example, in their extensive review of the literature, Carpenter and Armenti (1972) conclude that the relationship between the chemical action of alcohol and sexual desire has not been established. Experiments with animals and with humans have failed to demonstrate a positive relationship. Likewise, based on his analysis of the research, Brain (1986) refutes the view that alcohol simply switches on aggression in humans, and Wilson (1977), who strongly disputes the physiological disinhibition hypothesis, argues that in the research on disinhibition, correlation has been confused with cause—a problem that also plagues much rape research.

An alternative explanation for the alcohol-sexual violence correlation is that cultural expectations regulate the emotional consequences of drinking (Mandelbaum 1965), that disinhibition is learned behavior and points to the utility of drunkenness for deviance disavowal. MacAndrew and Edgerton (1969) provide strong evidence for this explanation in their classic anthropological study of "drunken comportment." In their analysis of cross-cultural data, they found a number of cultures in which people drink enormous quantities of hard alcohol, even to the point of passing out, but do not exhibit disinhibition. That is, people do not become more aggressive, do not exhibit increased sexual activity, and, in short, do not become creatures of impulse, doing things they ordinarily would not do as a result of alcohol consumption. On the other hand, there are also examples of cultures, ours included, in which people do change for the worse when drunk. To explain this contradictory behavior, MacAndrew and Edgerton argue that drunken comportment is learned and that it varies according to the situation. They state:

> Over the course of socialization, people learn about drunk-enness and what their society "knows" about drunken-ness; and, accepting and acting upon the understandings thus imparted to them, they become the living confirma-tion of their society's teachings. (p. 88)

Laboratory experiments provide further evidence that drunkenness is learned and that an individual's expectations about the effects of alcohol affect his or her behavior. In one such experiment, 96 male social drinkers were divided into two groups. One group was told they would be drinking vodka and tonic and the other group that they would be drinking tonic water only. Within each of these two groups, half of the men were actually given alcohol, while the other half were given only tonic. After drinking, half of the men were exposed to an insulting interaction involving a confederate of the researchers, while the control group was exposed to a neutral interaction. Then both groups were given the opportunity to aggress against the con-federate using a standard technique involving simulated electrical shock. Researchers found that the only significant determinant of aggression was the *expectation* of having consumed alcohol. Men who believed they had consumed alcohol were more aggressive than men who believed they had consumed tonic water, regardless of the actual alco-hol content of their drinks (Lang et al. 1975). In another experiment with the same design, researchers exposed men to erotic films depicting heterosexual intercourse and male homosexual interaction while measuring arousal as penile tumescence using a penile strain gauge. While researchers failed to find any effects of alcohol, they did find significant effects of expectation on sexual arousal. Men who believed they had consumed vodka manifested significantly greater sexual arousal than those who believed they had consumed tonic water, regardless of the actual content of their drinks (Wilson and Lawson 1976).

MacAndrew and Edgerton (1969) conclude that in cultures that display disinhibition, drunkenness represents "time-out behavior," in which individuals act in accord with the knowledge that they are exempted from the ordinary behavioral limits associated with sobriety. Although scant research has examined the question, observation suggests that there are gender differences in disinhibition and in drinking and drunken behavior. Unlike men, women do not seem to become violent toward others as a consequence of alcohol consumption. Noted one college counselor, women tend to become self-destructive rather than other-destructive (Welsh 1988), a pattern that is consistent with gender role expectations. However, when men are socialized to believe that they are not really themselves when drunk, it allows them to interpret drunken changes for the worse that result in violence as idiosyncratic, and not representative of their "true" selves. Thus, in societies like ours that display belief in and behavior associated with disinhibition, men can use drunkenness as an excuse for sexually violent behavior and to disclaim deviance. Supporting this observation, McCaghy (1968) found that male child molesters used alcohol as a technique for neutralizing their deviant identity, and, based on analysis of violent families, Coleman and Straus (1983) suggest that social learning and deviance disavowal provide a better understanding of the alcohol-violence relationship than does the disinhibition hypothesis. To date, however, the utility of alcohol as a method of neutralizing behavior has been discussed primarily with respect to its advantage as an excuse. The fact that alcohol and drugs can also be used as a justification for behavior has been largely ignored.

Indeed, whereas alcohol and drugs function to the advantage of sexually violent men, making them less responsible for their behavior, it is used to discredit the victims and to make them more responsible for the acts. For example,

LeGrand (1973) found that among the rape complaints filed by victims who had been drinking, 82 percent were classified unfounded. As one judge stated:

> When a woman drinks with a man to the point of intoxication, she practically invites him to take advantage of her person. She should not be permitted to yell when she is sober, "I was raped." (Ploscowe 1968, 215)

It was in the interest of admitters, who were attempting to excuse their behavior, to contend that alcohol and drugs had affected their behavior, and, if not the cause, they were at least a contributing factor. For example, an admitter who estimated his consumption to have been eight beers and four "hits of acid" reported:

> Straight, I don't have the guts to rape. I could fight a man but not that. To say, "I'm going to do it to a woman," knowing it will scare and hurt her, takes guts or you have to be sick.

Another admitter believed that alcohol

> brought out what was already there but in such intensity it was uncontrollable. Feelings of being dominant, powerful, using someone for my own gratification, all rose to the surface.

In contrast, deniers' justifications required they not be substantially impaired. To say that they had been drunk or high would cast doubt on their ability to control themselves or to remember events as they actually happened. Consistent with this, when asked if alcohol and/or drugs had had an effect on their behavior, 69 percent of admitters, but only 40 percent of deniers, said they had been affected.

Even more interesting was the way admitters and deniers constructed their victims' alcohol and drug use. Since admitters had already relieved themselves of responsibility through claims of being drunk or high, they had nothing to gain from the assertion that their victims had used or

124

been affected by alcohol and/or drugs. On the other hand, it was very much in the interest of deniers to declare that their victims had been intoxicated or high: that fact lessened victims' credibility and made victims themselves appear more responsible for the acts. Consistent with this observation, 72 percent of deniers but only 26 percent of admitters maintained that alcohol or drugs had been consumed by their victims. Further, while 56 percent of deniers declared their victims had been affected by this use, only 15 percent of admitters made a similar claim. Typically, deniers argued that the alcohol and drugs had sexually aroused their victims or rendered them out of control. For example, one denier insisted that his victim had become hysterical from drugs, not from being raped, and it was because of the drugs that she had reported him to the police. In addition, 40 percent of deniers argued that while the victim had been drunk or high, they themselves either had not ingested or were not affected by alcohol and/or drugs. In comparison, none of the admitters made this claim. In fact, in all of the 15 percent of cases where an admitter said the victim was drunk or high, he also admitted to being similarly affected.

These findings strongly suggest that sexually violent men have learned the advantage to be gained from using alcohol and drugs as an explanation for their behavior. These men clearly were aware that their victims would be discredited and their own behavior excused or justified by the self-interested portrayal of alcohol and drugs in their crimes.

The Sick Role

Echoing popular beliefs about rape, 40 percent of admitters said they thought an emotional problem had been at the root of their rape behavior, and 33 percent related the problem to an unhappy, unstable childhood or a marital-domestic situation. Still others claimed to have been in a general state of uneasiness. For example, one admitter said that at the time of the rape he had been depressed, feeling he couldn't do anything right, and that something had been missing from his life. But, he also added, "being a rapist is not part of my personality." Even admitters who could locate no source for an emotional problem evoked the popular image of rapists as sick to argue they also must have problems. For example:

> The fact that I'm a rapist makes me different. Rapists aren't all there. They have problems. It was wrong so there must be a reason why I did it. I must have a problem.

In fact, an upsetting event involving a problem of everyday living did precede the rapes of 80 percent of admitters and 25 percent of deniers. Groth (1979), likewise, found precipitating events among the incarcerated rapists in his clinical population. In contrast, as noted in Chapter 3, Smithyman (1978) found that his "undetected" rapists negotiated life events without problem. These seemingly contradictory findings may reflect differences in the two populations of rapists studied. Smithyman's "undetected" rapists, like deniers, saw nothing especially unusual about their behavior or themselves. As a prison psychologist, Groth observed men, like admitters, who relied on emotional problems to explain their behavior.

Of those men who experienced an upsetting event, including deniers, 76 percent of those events involved a wife or girlfriend. Again and again, these men described themselves as having been in a rage because of an incident involving a woman with whom they believed they were in love.[1] Reflecting their rigid "pedestal" attitudes (see Chapter 3), the event was frequently related to a double standard for sexual conduct and virtue that they applied to their women but that they didn't expect from men, didn't apply to themselves, and, obviously, didn't honor in other women. Discovering that the "pedestal" didn't apply to their wives or girlfriends sent them into a fury. One especially articulate admitter described his feelings in the following way. After serving a short prison term for auto theft, he married his "childhood sweetheart" and secured a well-paying job. Between his job and the volunteer work he was doing with an ex-offender group, he was spending long hours away from home, a situation that bothered his wife. In response to her request, he gave up his volunteer work, though it was clearly mean- ingful to him. Then, one day, he discovered his wife with her former boyfriend, "and my life fell apart." During the next several days, he said his anger intensified and caused him to withdraw into himself. After three days of drinking in a motel room, he abducted and raped a woman he didn't know. He stated:

> My parents have been married for many years and I had high expectations about marriage. I put my wife on a pedestal. When I walked in on her, I felt like my life had been destroyed, it was such a shock. I was bitter and angry about the fact that I hadn't done anything to my wife for cheating. I didn't want to hurt her [his victim], only to scare and degrade her.

It is clear that a number of these men were experiencing stress at the time of their rapes. But their problems were ordinary—the types of upsetting events that almost everyone experiences at some point in life. Since women and some men experience equally disturbing events but do not rape, these everyday stresses are hardly an adequate explanation for rape. Ultimately, the question that must be addressed is why some men choose sexual violence as a method of coping with their personal problems.

As with alcohol and drugs, emotional problems work differently depending upon whether the behavior in question is being justified or excused. It would have been counter- productive for deniers to claim they had emotional problems at the time of the rape because it would have cast suspicion on their ability to interpret events accurately. Admitters, how- ever, used psychological explanations to portray themselves as having been temporarily "sick" at the time of the rape. Sick people ordinarily are blamed for neither the cause of their illness nor for acts committed while in that state of diminished capacity. Thus, adopting the sick role removes responsibility by excusing the behavior as having been beyond the ability of the individual to control. Since these men claimed not to be "themselves," the rapes they committed were idiosyncratic rather than typical behavior. Admitters, then, could assert a nondeviant identity despite their self-proclaimed disgust with what they had done.

However, although admitters were willing to assume the sick role, they did not view their problems as a chronic condition, nor did they believe themselves to be insane or permanently impaired. Said one admitter, who believed that he needed psychological counseling, "I have a mental disorder, but I'm not crazy." Instead, admitters viewed their "problem" as mild, transient, and most definitely curable. Indeed, part of the appeal of this excuse is that it not only relieves responsibility, but, as with alcohol and drugs, allows men who rape to "recover"—in some cases, very quickly. It is not surprising, then, that at the time of their interviews the majority of admitters, 69 percent, like all of the deniers, were able to say that "being a rapist" was not part of their self-concept.

Nice Guy

Admitters attempted to neutralize their crimes further and negotiate a nonrapist identity by portraying themselves as essentially "nice guys." In contrast to the denier, whose bragging was aimed at asserting a lack of need to rape, the image projected by the admitter was that of someone who had made a serious mistake, but, in every other respect, was a decent guy. Indeed, when asked about their current feelings for their victims, 57 percent of admitters responded with expressions of regret and sorrow and indicated that they wished there were a way to apologize or make amends for their behavior. For example, a participant in a group rape-murder, who insisted his partner did the killing, confided:

> I wish there was something I could do besides saying, "I'm sorry, I'm sorry." I live with it 24 hours a day and sometimes, I wake up crying in the middle of the night.

An apology has significance beyond the obvious expression of guilt (Schlenker and Darby 1981). From the perspective of the person apologizing, it allows the admission of guilt along with an attempt to gain a pardon by convincing the audience that the event should not be considered a fair representation of what the person is really like. Thus, an apology separates the bad self from the good self and promises more acceptable future behavior. When apologizing, the individual is attempting to say, "I have repented and should be forgiven," thus making it appear that no further rehabilitation is necessary.

Admitters' "nice guy" statements reflected an attempt to communicate just such a message. First, they attempted to convey the idea that rape was not a representation of their "true" selves. For example:

> It's different from anything else I've ever done. I feel more guilt about this. It's not consistent with me. When I talk about it, it's like being assaulted myself. I don't know why I did it, but once I started, I got into it. Armed robbery was a way of life for me but not rape. I feel like I wasn't being myself.

Admitters also used "nice guy" statements to register their moral indignation toward violence and harming women, even though, in some cases, they had injured their own victims. Such was the case with an admitter convicted of a group rape, who insisted:

> I'm against hurting women. She should have resisted. None of us were the type of person that would use force on a woman. I never positioned myself on a woman unless she showed an interest in me. They played to me, not me to them. My weakness is to follow. I never would have stopped, let alone pick her up without the others. I never would have let anyone beat her. I never bothered women who didn't want sex: never had a problem with sex or getting it. I loved her—like all women.

Finally, a number of admitters attempted to improve their self-images by demonstrating that, while they had raped, it could have been worse if they had not been "nice guys." For example, one admitter professed to being especially gentle with his victim after she told him she had just had a baby.

129

Others claimed to have given their victims money to get home or to make a phone call, or to have made sure the victims' children were in a room where they would not witness the rape. A multiple rapist, whose pattern was to break in and attack sleeping women in their beds, stated:

> I never beat any of my victims and I told them I wouldn't hurt them if they cooperated. I'm a professional thief. But I never robbed the women I raped because I felt so bad about what I had already done to them.

Even a young man who abducted and raped his five victims at gunpoint and then stabbed them to death attempted to improve his image by asserting:

> Physically they enjoyed the sex [rape]. Once they got involved, it would be difficult to resist. I was always kind and gentle until I started to kill them. And the killing was always sudden, so they wouldn't know it was coming.

"A Dangerous and Vicious Animal"

Chapter 4 introduced the related concepts of reflexive and synesic role-taking: in rape, the processes by which a sexually violent man would see himself from his victim's perspective and imagine her feelings. Unlike deniers, who were incapable of role-taking, admitters used their facility for role-taking to accomplish and enjoy their rapes. Thus, while admitters played the role of "nice guy" at the time of their interviews, this was not the role they played when they raped.

Compared to the lack of self-awareness among deniers, very few admitters responded that they didn't know or didn't care when asked to describe how they thought their victims would have described them. Instead, the majority of admitters, 58 percent, demonstrated some amount of self-awareness and, additionally, used violent and negative images to describe themselves. For example, one man said:

130

Like an animal, like you would describe someone you
hated that was foul and disgusting—hideous is a good
way to put it.

And from another, "Vicious, threatening, unstable, breath-
ing heavy, eyes glazed over, crazy." Thus, the majority of
admitters did seem to see themselves from the perspective
of a woman victim. More precisely, they demonstrated the
ability to anticipate the perspective of real or imaginary
women in the role of their victim. Indeed, this awareness validated their self-image,[2] meaning that admitters'
perceptions of themselves reflected conformity to victims'
expected conceptions of rapists.

It is not possible to know whether admitters actually held
these perceptions at the time of their rapes or whether
they were the product of retrospective reflection and the
experience of being publicly labeled rapists.[3] Since feelings and perceptions obviously cannot be measured during
or even immediately following a rape, information is of
necessity based on retrospective accounts. It is relevant,
however, that deniers did not retrospectively reevaluate
themselves, although a few of the men did state that they
had changed from denial to admitting since coming to prison
(none indicated the reverse pattern). Even such a change,
however, does not preclude the ability to separate current
feelings and perceptions from those experienced at the time
of the rape. Thus, it must be assumed that the guiding
imagery for admitters' behavior was that of a dangerous,
violent, disgusting, demented animal. And even if this image
was influenced by cultural stereotypes, the consequences are
no less real or dangerous.

Emotions like guilt, shame, and embarrassment are the
expected outcome of seeing ourselves from the perspective
of the other. The self-image of a dangerous, violent animal,
however, did not produce these emotions in the majority of admitters at the time of the rape. When asked to
describe their feelings immediately after raping, 32 percent
of admitters responded they had felt scared or concerned
for their own well-being. Like deniers, the most frequent
response, given by 43 percent of admitters, was that they

had no feelings at all. Only 27 percent of admitters said they felt any guilt or shame for their actions. Indeed, at the time, rape had negligible effect on their lives or emotions, despite the trauma to their victims. For example, an admitter who had abducted his victim, a pregnant woman, in a shopping center parking lot commented:

> I thought about killing her but I couldn't do it. I wasn't too scared. I took her money and went to the ABC [liquor] store, bought some liquor and drank it all. Then I went home and watched TV, my girlfriend came over and I forgot about it.

Another admitter who had attacked his victim, a woman he claimed was a "known prostitute," when she came to his house selling magazines reported:

> It just blew past. I played some basketball and then went to my girl's house and had sex with her. I wasn't worried or sorry.

Thus, the overwhelming majority of these sexually violent men did not experience guilt or shame at the time of the rape as a result of their actions. For these men, the feeling rules that govern sexual violence called for emotional neutrality.

"Dirty and Degraded"

Admitters were not only self-aware, but were also able to imagine their victims' feelings during the rape—evidence of synesic role-taking. With few exceptions, admitters were able to describe their victims' immediate reactions upon understanding a rape was imminent and also to explain how they thought the victims had felt during and immediately after the rapes. Essentially they perceived their victims either as terrified and thus unable to resist or as resisting initially but becoming passive as a result of their intimidation by either a show of force or a weapon. For example, one victim was described as saying, "Don't hurt me, I'll do

132

what you want." And her rapist said, "She was trembling and afraid. There was no resistance or screams." A multiple rapist confided, "They were all scared to death and I liked that feeling of being totally dominant." And a multiple rapist-murderer admitted, "I terrified them by telling them I would kill them and cut them up in pieces." Based on these initial impressions, admitters could assume their victims would be passive and compliant during the rape. Having defined their victims as rapable and the situation as favorable, admitters were able to proceed with their plans of action.

Once established, their situational advantage made it less necessary for these men to focus on their victims' reactions. Nonetheless, only 21 percent of admitters indicated they didn't know or didn't care when asked how they thought their victims had felt during the rapes. Instead, the majority of admitters, 58 percent, gave some evidence of understanding rape from a victim's point of view. It is interesting that the most frequent description of victims' feelings, 46 percent of responses, consisted of inwardly directed emotions connected with powerlessness—that is, humiliation and degradation. Typical comments were, "I think she felt hurt, degraded, worthless because she was getting fucked," and, "I think she felt dirty, cheap, ashamed, and afraid of what others would say." By contrast, only 12 percent of admitters mentioned outwardly directed, more violent emotions, like anger and hate, to describe their victims' feelings. Perhaps they perceived their victims' powerlessness as so complete that they did not consider the possibility that the victims may have been experiencing such emotions. Selective perception may also have been involved. That is, admitters chose to emphasize the feelings related to the outcomes they wanted their actions to produce. As one admitter commented:

> I assume she felt degraded, angry, and used. The parts of her body that I touched felt dirty and that was just what I wanted.

The ability to understand their victims' experiences during the rapes, however, did not produce feelings of empathy. When asked to describe their feelings for their victims during

133

the rapes, the majority of admitters, 54 percent, like the majority of deniers, reported feeling nothing at all. For example, one admitter said, "I had no feelings at all, she was like an object." And from another, "I didn't feel anything. It was just something I was going to do." A small number of admitters expressed anger, hate, control, and domination. For example, a gang rapist reported:

> I felt macho and power over her. Maybe a little anger. I felt she was a dirty slut and anything we did was justified. It gave me a sense of status.

And finally, "I felt like I had put her in her place."

Excusing Sexual Violence

What, then, can be said about men who excuse rape? Admitters' accounts reveal the social factors that permit sexual violence to be excused. They are men who acknowledge they have raped and also express the belief that rape is morally reprehensible. Excuses were the device that allowed them to explain themselves and their acts in socially acceptable terms by appealing to forces beyond their control, forces that reduced their capacity to act rationally and thus compelled them to rape. These excuses—alcohol and drug use, and emotional problems—allowed them to view their rapes as idiosyncratic rather than typical behavior. Thus, they had made serious mistakes that did not represent their "true" selves. As evidence that they were actually "nice guys," most of the admitters expressed deep regret for their behavior and the desire to apologize to their victims. These, however, were not their sentiments at the time of the rapes.

It appears that patriarchal societies can produce imperceptive men like deniers, but also can produce aware men like admitters. Indeed, the majority of admitters demonstrated that they understood the generalized image women have of rapists. Consistent with that knowledge, their perception of themselves was that of violent and subhuman creatures, and they used that image to their advantage, believing they terrified their victims and rendered them subdued and compliant. Admitters were also aware of the emotional impact of rape on women. While raping, they took satisfaction in the belief that their victims felt powerless, humiliated, and degraded—the way they wanted their victims to feel. Indeed, admitters used their ability to role-take to enact sexual violence and to experience satisfaction from it.

Admitters and deniers were similar in one very important respect. The majority did not experience guilt or shame during or immediately following their rapes, nor did they report feeling empathy for their victims at that time. Instead of the emotions that might have constrained their sexually violent behavior, these men indicated that they felt nothing or they felt satisfied.

Chapters 4 and 5 have presented convicted rapists' social construction of sexual violence—a reality not shared by women. These chapters have shown how culture provides the excuses and justifications that allow men who rape to explain sexual violence in socially acceptable terms. Justifications, in particular, but also excuses, are buttressed by the cultural view of women as sexual objects, dehumanized, and lacking autonomy and dignity—a view that also allowed these men to rape without emotion. Through the skillful use of these justifications and excuses, deniers were able to define their behavior as wrong, but not rape, while admitters were able to view their behavior as rape, but not themselves as rapists. In the final analysis, whether or not they regarded their behavior as rape, the overwhelming majority claimed, "I'm not a rapist." The perspective of these men reduced rape to nothing and no one to a rapist. The next chapter will continue this exploration of sexually violent men by examining the functions of rape from their perspective.

Notes

1 The function that rape served for these men will be explored in Chapter 6.
2 For a discussion of this point, see Turner (1962).
3 Sociologists refer to such events as "degradation ceremonies"; Garfinkle (1956).

6

Rape: A Low-Risk, High-Reward Crime

What Men Gain from Sexual Violence

In this chapter, the purpose is to look deeper into rapists' construction of reality by examining the goals they learned to accomplish through sexually violent means. The distinction between admitters and deniers is not important here, as the objective is to focus on the essential question of what men gain from rape (regardless of their excuses and justifications) in a contemporary sexually violent society. This chapter will demonstrate that for many sexually violent men the motivations to rape are not irrational, subconscious, and uncontrollable but, rather, overt and deliberate. For some men, rape is used as a method of revenge and punishment; for others, it is a bonus added while committing another crime. In other cases, rape is used to gain sexual access to unwilling or unavailable women, and for some, it is a source of impersonal sex and power. Rape is also a form of recreation and adventure for some men and, finally, it is an act that makes them "feel good." Indeed, what these men tell us is that from their perspective, rape is a low-risk, high-reward act.

Revenge and Punishment

Donald Black (1983), a criminologist, suggests that it is theoretically useful to explore what criminal behavior has in common with other kinds of conduct. He argues that, when interpreted from the offender's perspective, crime, in modern societies, as in preindustrial or tribal societies, often is used as a form of "self-help"—a way to express a grievance through aggression and violence. The objective may be conflict management, punishment, or revenge. For example, in societies where women are the property of men, rape is sometimes used as a means of avenging oneself on the victim's husband or father, or it may be an institutionalized form of punishment for women (see Hoebel 1954; Llewellyn and Hoebel 1941).

When applied to rape, Black's approach is illuminating because it forces us to examine the uses to which sexual violence is put in our society and to acknowledge that some men who rape view their acts as a legitimate form of revenge or punishment. Also important is the idea of "collective liability," which Black argues accounts for much seemingly random violence—the type of rape that women appear to fear most. (See the Afterword for a discussion of fear of rape.) "Collective liability" suggests that all people in a particular category are held accountable for each of their counterparts. Thus, a man's intent may not be to punish the woman he is raping but to use her because she represents a category to him.

These factors—revenge, punishment, and the collective liability of women—can be used to explain a number of the rapes committed by the men in this research. Several examples will illustrate the ways in which these factors combined in various types of rapes. Revenge rapes were also especially brutal, involving a level of gratuitous violence that was far beyond what was necessary to accomplish the rape and often including beatings, serious injuries, and even murder.

Revenge rapes most often were preceded by an upsetting event involving a significant woman (for a full discussion, see Chapter 5). When they raped, these men were angry because of a perceived indiscretion, typically related to a rigid moralistic standard of sexual conduct that they required from "their women" but, in most cases, did not abide by themselves. Indeed, their anger was a violent expression of the "pedestal" double standard. Thus, the question posed in the last chapter—why these men sought to redress their personal problems through rape—is answered by the observation that over and over they talked about using rape "to get even" with their wives or significant women. Thus, the collective liability of women was a prominent feature of revenge rapes, as, from the rapists' perspective, their victims were substitutes for the women against whom they wanted to retaliate. Typical is a young man who, prior to the rape, had a violent argument with his wife over what eventually proved to be her misdiagnosed case of venereal disease. She assumed the disease had been contracted through him, an accusation that infuriated him. After fighting with his wife, he explained that he drove around "thinking about hurting someone." He encountered his victim, a stranger, on the road, where her car had broken down. It appears she accepted his offered ride because her car was out of commission. When she realized that a rape was imminent, she called him "a son of a bitch," and attempted to resist. He reported flying into a rage and beating her, and he confided:

> I have never felt that much anger before. If she had resisted, I would have killed her. . . . The rape was for revenge. I didn't have an orgasm. She was there to get my hostile feelings off on.

Although not the most common form of revenge rape, sexual violence appears to be used by some men as a form of retaliation against the victim's male partner. In one such case, the man, angry because the victim's husband owed him money, went to the victim's house to collect. He confided, "I was going to get it one way or another." Finding the victim alone, he explained, they started to argue about the money, and

> I grabbed her and started beating the hell out of her. Then I committed the act. I knew what I was doing. I was mad. I could have stopped but I didn't. I did it to get even with her and her husband.

As Griffin (1971) points out, when women are viewed as commodities, "In raping another man's woman, a man may

139

aggrandize his own manhood and concurrently reduce that of another man."

Revenge rapes often also included the intent to punish. In some cases, while the victim was not the initial object of the revenge, the intent was to punish her because of something that transpired after the decision to rape had been made or during the course of the rape itself. This was the case with a young man whose wife had recently left him. Although they were in the process of reconciliation, he remained angry and upset over the separation. The night of the rape, he met the victim and her friend in a bar where he had gone to watch a fight on television. The two women apparently accepted a ride from him, but, after taking her friend home, he drove the victim to his apartment. At his apartment, the victim allegedly made a sexual remark about his dog that, he reported, put him in a rage. In the ensuing attack, he raped and pistol whipped the victim. Then he forced a vacuum cleaner hose, switched on suction, into her vagina and bit her breast, severing the nipple. He stated:

I hated at the time, but I don't know if it was her [the victim]. [Who could it have been?] My wife? Even though we were getting back together, I still didn't trust her.

During his interview it became clear that, like many sexually violent men, he believed men have the right to discipline and punish women. In fact, he self-righteously defended himself by arguing that most of the men he knew also would have beaten the victim because "that kind of thing [referring to the dog] is not acceptable among my friends." Notice that the dog is accorded more rights than the woman.

Finally, in some rapes, both revenge and punishment were directed at victims because they represented women in general whom these men perceived as collectively responsible and liable for their problems. Rape was used "to put women in their place" and as a method of proving their "manhood" by displaying dominance over a woman. For example, one multiple rapist believed that his actions were related to the feeling that women thought they were better than he was:

Rape was a feeling of total dominance. Before the rapes, I would always get a feeling of power and anger. I would degrade women so that I could feel there was a person of less worth than me.

For this type of man, rape may represent a "safer" form of "self-help" than violence against another male, who would pose a physically more threatening target.

Another, especially brutal, example involved a young man from an upper-middle-class background, who spilled out his story in a seven-hour interview conducted in his solitary-confinement cell. He described himself as tremendously angry, at the time, with his girlfriend, who he believed was involved with him in a "storybook romance," and from whom he expected complete fidelity. When she went away to college and became involved with another man, his revenge lasted 18 months and involved the rape and murder of five women, all strangers who lived in his community. Explaining his rape-murders, he stated:

I wanted to take my anger and frustration out on a stranger, to be in control, to do what I wanted to do. I wanted to use and abuse someone as I felt used and abused. I was killing my girlfriend. During the rapes and murders, I would think about my girlfriend. I hated the victims because they probably messed men over. I hated women because they were deceitful and I was getting revenge for what happened to me.

An Added Bonus

Burglary and robbery commonly accompany rape. Indeed, among the rapists interviewed, 39 percent had also been convicted of one or the other of these crimes committed in connection with their rapes. In some cases, the original intent was rape and robbery was an afterthought—the most familiar pattern. However, in this research, a surprising number of the men indicated that the reverse pattern was true in their cases. That is, the decision to rape was made subsequent to their original intent, which was burglary or robbery.

Such was the case with a young man who stated that he originally intended only to rob the store in which his victim happened to be working. He explained that when he found the victim alone,

> I decided to rape her to prove I had guts. She was just there. It could have been anybody.

Indeed, a number of the men indicated that the decision to rape had been made after they realized they were in control of the situation. This was true of an unemployed offender who confided that his practice was to steal whenever he needed money. On the day of the rape, he drove to a local supermarket and paced the parking lot, "staking out the situation." His pregnant victim was the first person to come along alone and "she was an easy target." Threatening her with a knife, he reported the woman as saying she would do anything if he didn't harm her. At that point, he decided to force her to drive to a deserted area, where he raped her. He explained:

> I wasn't thinking about sex. But when she said she would do anything not to get hurt, probably because she was pregnant, I thought, "why not."

The attitude of these men toward rape was similar to their attitude toward burglary and robbery. Quite simply, if the situation is right, "why not." Thus, while the psychiatric perspective attempts to differentiate rape as a special "disease," from the perspective of these men, rape was just another part of their ordinary routine—an added bonus.

Sexual Access

In an effort to change public attitudes that are damaging to the victims of rape and to reform laws seemingly premised on the assumption that women both ask for and enjoy rape, the feminist position has emphasized the violent and aggressive character of rape. Often these arguments disclaim that sex plays any part in rape at all.[1] This contrasts with the psychopathological position, which emphasizes the sexual nature of rape and ignores the violence. I argue, however, that both positions miss the mark. Rape is a violent act, but it is also a sexual act, and it is this fact that differentiates it from other crimes. Further, it is illogical to argue, on the one hand, that rape is an extension of normative male sexual behavior and, on the other hand, that rape is not sexual. As MacKinnon (1983) correctly observes, rape is not less sexual for being violent, nor is it necessarily true that the violent aspect of rape distinguishes it from legally "acceptable" intercourse. For example, marital rape is not legally recognized in most of the United States. It is unfortunate that the rather swift public acceptance of the "rape as violence" model, even among groups who otherwise discount feminist arguments, has unintended implications. For example, I have heard the rape as violence argument used by advocates of pornography to deny any link between pornography and rape. Equally important, emphasizing violence—the victims' experience—is also strategic to the continued avoidance of an association between "normal" men and sexual violence. Make no mistake, for some men, rape is sex—in fact, for them, sex is rape. The continued rejection of this possibility, threatening though it may be, is counterproductive to understanding the social causes of sexual violence.

In his study of rapists, Groth (1979) attributes a psychodynamic function to sex in rape, arguing that rapists' aggressive needs are expressed through sexuality. In other words, rape is a means to an end. I argue, however, that from the rapists' point of view, rape is in part sexual, that men who rape view the act as an end in itself, and that sexual access most obviously demonstrates the link between sex and rape. Rape as a means of sexual access also illuminates the deliberate nature of this act. When a woman is unwilling or seems unavailable for sex, men can use rape to seize what is not offered. In discussing his decision to rape, one man made this clear:

All the guys wanted to fuck her . . . a real fox, beautiful shape. She was a beautiful woman and I wanted to see what she had.

The view of sex as a male entitlement suggests that when a woman says no, rape is a suitable method of conquering the "offending" object. If, for example, a woman is picked up at a party, in a bar, or while hitchhiking—behavior that a number of these men saw as a signal of sexual availability—and she later resists sexual advances, rape is presumed to be justified. The same justification operates in what is popularly called "date rape." The belief that sex was their just compensation compelled a number of rapists to insist they had not raped. In other words, from the perspective of these men, rape depends on whether they, not their victims, perceive a violation. MacKinnon (1983) points out that rape laws operate on a similar basis, allowing men's conditioned unconsciousness to counterindicate women's experience of violation. Consider the case of a man who raped and seriously beat his victim when, on their second date, she refused his sexual advances.

> I think I was really pissed off at her because it didn't go as planned. I could have been with someone else. She led me on but wouldn't deliver. . . . I have a male ego that must be fed.

His goal was conquest, to seize what was not offered, and, like others, he believed his behavior was justified.

Sexual access was also a motivation in the accounts of several men who deliberately chose a victim because she was relatively older than they were. These men were themselves rather young, 26 to 30 years of age at the time of interview, and they chose victims older than themselves because they believed that sexually experienced women were more desirable partners. They raped because they also believed that these women would not be sexually attracted to them. Thus, through rape they gained access to unattainable women.

Finally, sexual access emerged as a factor in the accounts of some black men who raped white women—a topic that requires some introductory elaboration. Since the beginning of the antirape movement in the 1960s, activists have tended to avoid this topic. Contributing to the silence is an acute awareness of historical and contemporary social injustice.

144

Davis (1981), for example, points out that during slavery, the rape of black women by white men was virtually institutionalized in the South and that the fictional rape of white women was used as a postslavery justification to lynch black men.[2] Indeed, prior to the Civil War, rape laws were explicitly racist in many states. In Georgia, for example, capital punishment was mandated when a black man was convicted of the rape or attempted rape of a white woman, while the penalty for white men convicted of raping black women was a fine, prison, or both, at the discretion of the court (LaFree 1989). Consistent with this differential treatment, of the 453 men executed for rape in the United States since 1930, 405 of them, or 89 percent, have been black (LaFree 1989, 141). And LaFree's (1989) research demonstrates that black men charged with raping white women continue to be treated more harshly in the criminal justice system than black men charged with raping black women (see also LaFree 1980). While silence has been defensible in light of historic racial injustice, continued avoidance of analyzing intraracial rape ultimately harms women of all races by removing the opportunity to investigate the impact of social factors on sexual violence.

The majority of rapes in the United States are intraracial— white men primarily rape white women and men of color primarily rape women of color. However, for the past 20 years, according to national data based on reported and unreported rapes, the rate of black on white (B/W) rape has significantly exceeded the rate of white on black (W/B) rape. Indeed, assuming the data are correct, we are experiencing a historical anomaly, since white men have a long history of raping black women and other women of color at home and elsewhere, during peace and during war (Brownmiller 1975; Davis 1981). Linda Brent's recently reprinted *Incidents in the Life of a Slave Girl* (1973), for example, is compelling testimony to horrors that black women and girls suffered at the hands of their white slave masters and to the complicity of their white mistresses.

LaFree (1982) is one of the few social scientists who has investigated interracial rape. Justifying his efforts, in light of historical racism, LaFree (1982) points out that failure to consider race differences in rape hinders the development of a theory that explains rape in terms of general relationships between men and women, rather than individual motives of rapists.

Utilizing data from 19 separate empirical studies of reported rapes dating back to 1958, LaFree demonstrates that during the last two decades, the reported rate of B/W rape has increased, with the rate of these reportings never falling below 12.9 percent since 1967. Reported rape rates are problematic because they may contain systematic bias. For example, a white woman may be more likely to report a rape involving a black man. Similarly, fearing racist treatment, black women might be less willing than white women to report rape, regardless of the race of the attacker. However, data from national victimization studies, which include unreported rapes, show a pattern similar to reported rape.

Through surveys of scientifically selected households in the United States conducted by the Department of Justice, Law Enforcement Assistance Administration, during the years 1973 through 1977, data on crime victimization were collected. It should be pointed out that despite scientific techniques, black households may have been undersampled in this research for a number of social reasons, for example, possible reluctance of interviewers to enter certain areas or buildings. Occupants of the households surveyed were interviewed about their experience as victims of reported and *unreported* crime. The purpose of the studies was to determine the extent and characteristics of unreported crime, including rape. LaFree's analysis of the victimization data reveals that from 1973 through 1977, rates of B/W rape varied from 30.4 percent in 1973, to 12.9 percent in 1975, to 24.4 percent in 1977. Rates of W/B rape varied from 0.0 in 1973, to 2.6 percent in 1975, to 6.7 percent in 1977. LaFree (1982, 314) concludes, "Combining the yearly results from 1963 through 1977, B/W rapes were ten times more likely than W/B rapes."

Among the black men in this research, 66 percent reported that their victims were white, compared to two white men who reported raping black women. While this pattern is in the direction of the national data, these figures cannot be interpreted as an accurate reflection of the racial composition of rapes committed in this state or elsewhere. In addition to bias in rape reporting and processing, since black men who assault white women receive more serious sanctions within the criminal justice system when compared to other racial combinations of victim and assailant, B/W rape will be overrepresented within prison populations as well as overrepresented in any sample drawn from the population. (For other limitations of the sample, see Chapter 1.) In choosing the sample for this research, careful attention was paid to interviewing roughly equal numbers of white and black men. However, the races of victims were not known when the sample was chosen, although they were verified by record checks after the interview. All that can be concluded is that a relatively large proportion of black men who raped white women volunteered to be interviewed. The task here is to understand the social factors that contribute to this pattern of rape.

LaFree's (1982) purpose in analyzing the victimization data was to explore two models that might explain the increased rates of B/W rape. On the one hand, he reasoned, the increase may be the precursor of changing normative patterns allowing more interracial contact—a "normative model" (p. 314). This model would predict that B/W rapes should involve acquaintances, incidents that occur in the victims' homes, incidents where the offender had a right to be at the scene of the offense, and assaults by a lone offender. In contrast, a "conflict model" would explain interracial rape in terms of sexual access to a scarce resource and a challenge to white authority (p. 315). In this case, the rapes should involve strangers, incidents away from the victims' homes, incidents where the offender had no right to be at the scene, weapons, and more violence and injury than the normative model would predict.

Analyzing a sample of 453 rapes from the victimization studies, Lafree rejected the normative model for a modified conflict model. B/W rapes were more likely to involve strangers and to occur away from victims' homes, but they were no more violent than other rapes, suggesting that sexual access, rather than a political act, was intended.

Again, the pattern of B/W rapes in this research was similar to that shown in the national data. According to their records, 78 percent of the black rapists in our sample chose white victims who were strangers, and 65 percent of the rapes involved weapons. Some of the men declined to discuss their choice of white victims, although they were willing to discuss other aspects of their crimes. Those who did discuss their victims' race fit the modified conflict model. Sexual access to white women, not racial hostility, was the most common theme. Sexual curiosity about white women was evident in these interviews—a curiosity no doubt stimulated by the excessive images of white women as sex objects projected by the dominant white male culture. Blocked by racial barriers from normal access, these men used rape to gain access to unavailable white women.[3] In a few cases, the decision to rape was made during the course of a burglary, a common pattern among white rapists as well. Finding the victim asleep, as one man put it, he decided to use the opportunity "to satisfy the urge to go to bed with a white woman to see if it was different." Raping white women was variously described as "the ultimate experience" and "a feeling of status, power, macho." For another man, raping a white woman had a special appeal because it violated a "known taboo," making it more dangerous and, thus, more exciting to him than raping a black woman.

This analysis suggests that contemporary interracial rape reflects patterns of race and gender relations in several ways. First, while women as a class have less power and social status than men as a class, black and other women of color are relatively more disadvantaged in the United States because they are subordinated by race and sex. Prejudice, segregation, and other factors continue to militate against interracial relationships. Thus the desire for access to the unavailable sex objects of white men (and perhaps by extension the white power structure) may be an important function in B/W rape, but it is not a motivation for white men to rape black women. Demographic and geographic barriers also interact to lower the incidence of W/B rape. Segregation as well as expected poverty in some black neighborhoods undoubtedly discourage some white men from choosing such areas as a target for burglary or robbery, so the number of rapes that would occur in this context also is reduced. Thus, shifting social conditions have changed the patterns of interracial rape in the United States.

Before leaving this topic, it is relevant to note the relationship between race and rape denial. Overall, a slightly larger proportion of black men than white men denied rape. However, black men were more likely to deny rape, while admitting sexual contact, when their victims were black. Of the rapes involving black victims, 79 percent were denied; in contrast, 59 percent of rapes involving white victims were denied. One plausible explanation is that black men find it more socially permissible to justify rape when the victim is black, especially if they know that the criminal justice system also perceives these crimes as less serious than when the victim is white. They may be aware that it would be less acceptable for them to blame a white woman or to suggest that she precipitated a rape involving a black man. Alternatively, it is possible that internalized racism, the pervasive cultural devaluation of black life, and negative stereotypes of black women result in some black men regarding the rape of a black woman as a relatively minor offense. Whatever the answer, it is clear that the historical and contemporary combination of racism and sexism has resulted in especially vicious victimization of black women.

Impersonal Sex, Rape Fantasy, and Pornography

The idea that rape is impersonal rather than intimate or mutual appealed to a number of rapists, some of whom suggested that it was their preferred form of sex. The fact that rape gave them the power to control and dominate their victims encouraged some to act on this preference. For example, one man explained:

> Rape gave me the power to do what I wanted to do without feeling I had to please a partner or respond to a partner. I felt in control, dominant. Rape was the ability

to have sex without caring about the woman's response. I was totally dominant.

Another rapist commented:

Seeing them laying there helpless gave me the confidence that I could do it. . . . With rape I felt totally in charge. I'm bashful, timid. When a woman wanted to give in normal sex, I was intimidated. In the rapes, I was totally in command, she totally submissive.

Although the men were not systematically questioned about their fantasies, one man volunteered that he had been fantasizing about rape for several weeks before committing his offense. He confided that he thought it would be "an exciting experience—a new high." Most appealing to him was the idea that he could make his victim "do it all for him" and that he would be in control. He fantasized that she "would submit totally and that I could have anything I wanted." Eventually he decided to act because his older brother told him "forced sex is great, I wouldn't get caught, and, besides, women love it." Though now he admits to his crime, he continues to believe his victim "enjoyed it."

Interestingly, most of the conjecture about fantasies of rape has been focused on women and can be attributed to Freud's early pronouncements on women's alleged masochistic need to be violated. However, despite the male proclivity toward sexual violence, considerably less attention has been focused on men's fantasies of doing the rape. Clearly, male rape fantasy is not confined to men behind bars.

In her book, *About Men*, Chesler (1978) notes that rape and other common pornography themes are the substance of male sexual fantasy. She comments:

Upon being asked about their sexual fantasies, many men describe pornographic scenes of disembodied, face-less, impersonal body parts: breasts, legs, vaginas, but-tocks. Men of all ages fantasize, voyeuristically, scenes of whorehouses and male gang rapes; scenes of rape and mutilation; scenes of seduction and strangling. (p. 228)

Recent research has consistently confirmed that fantasies of raping are relatively common among men, although frequency may differ as a function of other variables, such as age (see Hunt 1974; Pietropinto and Simenauer 1977). From the scant research that has been done, it appears that, consistent with actual accounts of men who do rape, the appeal of impersonal sex and the desire to dominate a woman is a major component of men's rape fantasies. Additionally, these fantasies usually include arousal of the woman being raped, which, as Chapter 4 demonstrates, is also a major category of justification for men who rape. Indeed, in analyzing rapists' accounts, one is struck by the parallels among these accounts, male rape fantasies, and the major themes depicted in violent pornography. This raises the critical issue of the types and directions of relationships among violent pornography, rape fantasy, and sexual aggression.

A growing body of literature points to a positive relationship between exposure to violent pornography and increases in the tendency toward sexual aggression under controlled laboratory conditions. The number of such experiments contained in the scientific literature is quite large. Almost all utilize college students and, for the most part, report similar findings. Thus, in the interest of brevity, the relevant work of two of the most prominent researchers in this field will be reviewed.

In one of the few experiments that examines the effect of sexually violent stimuli on male rape fantasy, Malamuth (1981b) randomly exposed male college students, classified as either sexually force oriented or non-force oriented according to questionnaire response, to rape or to mutually consenting versions of a slide audio show. The students then were instructed to create their own fantasies and to self-report their sexual arousal (found to correlate highly with physiological measures of arousal). Among the more significant findings was that those students exposed to the rape condition, regardless of their sexual force classification, created more violent sexual fantasies than those exposed to the mutually consenting version. Malamuth expresses concern about the possibility that violent fantasies may be stimulated by mass media exposure. Regarding the possible undesirable effects of violent rape fantasies, he notes the consistent findings that arousal to sexually violent stimuli is related to callous attitudes toward rape and rape victims and to self-reports of the possibility of raping (p. 44).

In another important series of experiments, Malamuth and his colleagues exposed male and female college students to descriptions of sexual intercourse in which a number of conditions had been manipulated (Malamuth, Haber, and Feshbach 1980; Malamuth, Heim, and Feshback 1980). Thus, rape, intent, amount of pain, amount of aggression, and the victim's sexual response were varied. Students next were asked to respond to a number of scale items measuring self-reports of mood and sexual arousal. The researchers found that while both males and females reported relatively high levels of arousal when the victim was depicted as experiencing an involuntary orgasm, there were also important gender differences. Men were highly aroused when the victim experienced an orgasm and pain; for the women, arousal was high when the victim experienced an orgasm and *no* pain. Malamuth et al. suggest that, for men, the appeal of pain and orgasm may be the idea of forcing a woman to climax, despite her pain and abhorrence of the assailant, which casts the rapist in a position of power. In so doing, the rapist has gained ultimate control over the only source of power historically associated with a woman—her body. In another elaborate series of experiments, Malamuth et al. (1986) found that aggression enhanced the sexual arousal of male college students who were aroused by depictions of forced sex. In addition, the higher the arousal to forced sex, the more accepting these men were of an ideology that justifies male aggression against and dominance over women and the greater the likelihood they self-reported the possibility of engaging in such acts in the future.

Donnerstein and his colleagues also examined the relationship between aggressive-erotic stimuli and aggressive responses toward women in a series of experiments in which male college students were initially exposed to one of two conditions: one group was angered by, and another group was treated in a neutral manner by, either a male or female research confederate (see Donnerstein 1980; Donnerstein and

Barrett 1978; Donnerstein and Hallam 1978; Donnerstein et al. 1975). The men were next shown a neutral, an erotic, or an aggressive-erotic film. Finally, they were given an opportunity to aggress against the male or female confederate by delivering an electric shock that was simulated but that the research participants thought was real. Researchers found that the aggressive-erotic film increased aggression overall and produced the highest increase in aggression against the female confederate. Further, the combination of the anger condition and arousal from the film produced the highest level of aggression against the female, but, even in the nonanger condition, aggression was increased. Noting that the men's association of the female confederate with the victim in the film was an important contributor to the aggression they directed toward her, Donnerstein and his colleagues conclude that aggressive-erotic stimuli can lead to increased aggressive behavior toward women.

More research is needed before absolute conclusions can be drawn. Nonetheless, these data do suggest that exposure to a fusion of sexuality and violence, particularly when combined with high levels of sexual arousal, should be a matter of concern. That is, the stimulation of sexual arousal within a violent context may result in a conditioning process in which violent acts become associated with sexual pleasure. Additionally, these data clearly point to the victims' arousal, a common theme in pornographic depictions of rape, as an important component of the appeal of such stimuli. The findings also shed light on the observation that convicted rapists derived pleasure from their sexual violence and help to explain why it was important for them to insist that their victims "enjoyed themselves."

This research, however, does not prove a causal relationship between pornography and actual rape, nor does it examine the effect of long-term exposure to depictions of sexual violence particularly on adolescents, the group that may be the most vulnerable to such material. Ethical considerations, however, make it unlikely that such investigations will ever be carried out, since there is reason to believe that such experiments could have damaging antisocial effects on the participants that could not be reversed. Nonetheless, researchers eventually will have to find innovative ways to move out of the experimental laboratory and beyond the world of male college students to discover what, if any, relationship exists between patterns of pornographic consumption and actual sexually aggressive or violent behaviors. To date, such pivotal investigations have yet to be done.

Although the focus of this research was not on pornography, an attempt, albeit limited, was made to gauge rapists' consumption of pornographic materials. Thus, both rapists and those in the control group of other felons were asked, "Before coming to prison, on average how often did you use pornographic or sexually explicit magazines, books, or movies?" The range of possible responses was "often," "sometimes," "seldom," or "never." An analysis of responses reveals that 65.3 percent of rapists, compared to 56.7 percent of the control group, indicated they had used pornography. Additionally, rapists used pornography somewhat more frequently than controls—29.5 percent of rapists responded "often" or "sometimes," compared to 22.7 percent of the control group. Unfortunately, these data are limited and suffer from a number of problems; they must be interpreted with caution. First, it is not necessary to use pornography to be influenced by the images of woman abuse that it projects, because it is only one, although the most violent and extreme, of the many cultural media that communicate such messages (for a discussion of this point, see Chapter 2). Additionally, the question asked in this research failed to distinguish between erotica and violent pornography, and it did not attempt to connect usage with later aggressive sexual behavior. Finally, it became clear midway through the research, when it was too late to change the wording, that the men were interpreting the question in a very literal sense, to mean "use" to achieve orgasm while masturbating. Had the word *view* been substituted for *use*, it is quite likely that the reports of both groups would have been higher. Nonetheless, these data do establish that the majority of convicted rapists were familiar with pornography and that their use of such material was somewhat greater than that of other felons.

Given the state of knowledge, what can be said about the link between exposure to sexually violent material and sexual aggression? Malamuth and Briere (1986) propose a multilevel model that posits that cultural factors and individual experiences influence intermediate variables, which consist of belief systems, sexual arousal to aggression, dominance and hostility toward women, personality characteristics, and social networks of aggressive supportive peers. These variables interact with situational conditions—opportunity and access, disinhibiting events, acute arousal, and priming stimuli such as pornography—to produce a potential array of antisocial behaviors against women that might be expressed in a variety of forms, such as denial of aggression as a crime, laboratory aggression, or nonviolent antisocial acts such as discrimination against women.

Likewise, my concern is with the indirect relationship between violent pornography and rape. That is, I would argue that the more cultural support within a society for hostile and aggressive acts toward women, the more likely such acts are to occur in that society for several reasons. We know that fantasies of raping women are somewhat common among men and that these fantasies share a thematic similarity with rapists' accounts and violent pornography. It is reasonable, then, to expect that the proliferation of cultural products, like pornography, intensifies the quantity and quality of violence in men's fantasies. Further, particularly when women are depicted as receiving pleasure from the violence directed at them, pornography trivializes rape and, thus, may encourage more men to act on their fantasies. Armed with the myths celebrated in violent pornography, such as women secretly want to be raped, men who rape can and do believe that their behavior is within the normative boundaries of the culture. As this book has demonstrated, the stronger the belief in rape myths, the less reprehensible sexually aggressive behavior becomes. In any case, until such time as research disproves these possibilities, they cannot be rejected and should be a matter of grave concern.

Recreation and Adventure

For some men, rape represented recreation and adventure. This was especially true among gang rapists, most of whom were young, in high school or of high school age, when convicted. Indeed, rape was just another form of delinquent activity, a rite of passage, and a male bonding activity. Part of the appeal was the sense of male camaraderie engendered by participating collectively in a dangerous activity. To prove oneself capable of "performing" under these circumstances was a substantial challenge and also a source of reward. One gang rapist articulated this feeling very clearly:

> We felt powerful, we were in control. I wanted sex and there was peer pressure. She wasn't like a person, no personalty, just domination on my part. Just to show I could do it—you know, macho.

Several forms of gang rape were revealed in this research. A common pattern was hitchhike-abduction rape. In these cases, the gang, cruising an area, "looking for girls," picked up a female hitchhiker for the purpose of having sex. Though the intent was rape, a number of the men did not view it as such because they believed that women hitchhiked primarily to signal sexual availability and only secondarily as a form of transportation. In these cases, the unsuspecting victim was driven to a deserted area, raped, and in the majority of cases physically injured. Sometimes the victim was not hitchhiking; she was abducted at knife point or gunpoint from the street, usually at night. Some of the men did not view this type of attack as rape either, because they believed that women who walk alone at night are prostitutes, and, of course, prostitutes have no rights. Additionally, they were usually convinced "she enjoyed it."

"Gang date" rape was another popular variation. In this pattern, one member of the gang would make a date with the victim. Then, without her knowledge or consent, she would be driven to a predetermined location and forcibly raped by each member of the group. One young man revealed that this practice was so much a part of his friends' recreational routine that they had rented a house for the purpose. From his perspective, the rape was justified because "usually the girl had a bad reputation, or we knew it was what she liked."

During his interview, another young man confessed to participating in 20 or 30 such "gang date" rapes because his driver's license had been revoked, making it difficult for him to "get girls." He claimed that 60 percent of the time, "they were girls known to do this kind of thing," but "frequently, the girls didn't want to have sex with all of us." In such cases, he said, "It might start out as rape but, then, they [the woman] would quiet down and none ever reported it to the police." He was convicted for a gang rape, which he described as "the ultimate thing I ever did," because, unlike his other rapes, the victim, in this case, was a stranger whom the group abducted as she walked home from the library. He felt that the group's past experience with "gang date" rape had prepared them for this crime in which the victim was blindfolded and driven to the mountains, where, though it was winter, she was forced to remove her clothing. Lying on the snow, she was raped by each of the men several times before being abandoned near a farm house. This young man continued to believe that if he had spent the night with her, rather than abandoning her, she would not have reported to the police.

It is important to note that the gang rapes in this study were especially brutal and violent, resulting in physical injury, even death. It is frightening to imagine the number of high school-age hitchhike-abduction and "gang date" rapes that are never reported, or, if reported, are not processed because of the tendency to disbelieve the victims of such rapes unless extensive injury accompanies the crime. The scope of this male "recreational" attack on girls and women is chilling, indeed.

Solitary rapists also used terms like "exciting," "a challenge," and "an adventure" to describe their feelings about rape. Like the gang rapists, these men found the element of danger made rape all the more exciting. Typifying this attitude was one man who described his rape as intentional. He reported:

It was exciting to get away with it [rape], just being able to beat the system, not women. It was like doing something illegal and getting away with it.

Another rapist confided that for him "rape was just more exciting and compelling" than a normal sexual encounter because it involved forcing a stranger. A multiple rapist asserted, "it was the excitement and fear and the drama that made rape a big kick."

Feeling Good

At the time of their interviews, some of the rapists, notably admitters, did express regret for their crimes. The experience of being convicted, sentenced, and incarcerated for rape undoubtedly produced many, if not most, of these feelings. What is clear is that, in contrast to the well-documented severity of the immediate impact and, in some cases, the long-term trauma experienced by the victims of sexual violence, the immediate emotional impact on the men was slight.

In fact, a number of the men volunteered the information that raping had a positive impact on their feelings. Feeling good or nothing at all about raping women is not an aberration limited to men in prison. In his study of "undetected rapists" (rapists outside of prison), Smithyman (1978) found that raping women had no impact on the rapists' lives, nor did it have a negative effect on their self-images.

For some men the satisfaction was in revenge. For example, a rapist and murderer of five women explained:

It seems like so much bitterness and tension had built up and this released it. It felt like I had just climbed a mountain and now I could look back.

Another man characterized rape as habit forming: "Rape is like smoking. You can't stop once you start," he confided. Finally, one man expressed the sentiments of many rapists when he stated:

After rape, I always felt like I had just conquered something, like I had just ridden the bull at Gilley's.

Rape: Some Men's Pleasure

As promised, this chapter has presented a perspective on sexual violence from the point of view of men who rape. Through their interviews, they have told us what they gained from their behavior and the objectives they learned to accomplish through sexually violent means, and they talked about the pleasures of raping.

These data demonstrate that men rape not because they are idiosyncratic or irrational, but because they have learned that in this culture sexual violence is rewarding. It is also significant that the overwhelming majority of these men stated that they never thought they would be punished for what they did. As one man put it,

> I knew what I was doing. I just said, the hell with the consequences. I told myself what I was going to do was rape . . . but I didn't think I would go to prison. I thought I had gotten away with it.

Some men took precautions against leaving evidence, for example, by withdrawing prior to ejaculation. Some did not fear prison because they did not define their behavior as rape. Still others knew that women frequently do not report rape and, of those cases that are reported, conviction rates are low. One man explained:

> At the time I didn't think of it as rape, just fucking, but I knew I was doing wrong. But I also knew most women don't report rape and I didn't think she would either.

Indeed, these men felt secure in their sexual violence. For them, rape was a rewarding, low-risk act. Understanding that otherwise normal men can and do rape is critical to the reduction of sexual violence against women. It forces us to inquire about what men are doing about *their* problem, an issue addressed in the next chapter.

Notes

1   For an example of this type of bipolar thinking, see Gilmartin-Zena (1988).
2   Davis also argues that "the resurgence of racism during the mid-1970s has been accompanied by a resurrection of the myth of the black rapist" (p. 196). She links this to "the insidious work of racist ideology" and to a failure of antirape theorists to identify the enormous number of (white) anonymous rapists who remain unreported, untried, and unconvicted (p. 199). Davis's discussion must be understood, as I think it was intended, to place rape within the context of historical racial injustice in the United States. Yet I am disappointed because, in an effort to support black men, Davis has taken a position no more defensible than that of those who believe that all rapists are black. Ultimately, such myopia victimizes women. If Davis is understood to argue that the black rapist is a myth, why should arresting officers, prosecuting attorneys, judges, and juries take seriously any woman, including a black woman, who charges a black man with rape?
3   Hernton (1965) seems to support this analysis observing that the sexualization of racism means that black men desire white women because they are a forbidden mythological symbol of womanhood, a symbol, I would add, created by white men.

7

Isn't Rape Men's Problem?

Cultural Origins of the Motivation to Rape

Shortly after his election to the presidency, George Bush gave a speech to an assembly of the American Association of University Women in which he strongly condemned violence against women. The next day at a news conference, referring to the AAUW speech, a woman reporter asked the president if he intended to give such a message to gatherings of men. Women, she correctly observed, already know about violence against them. We don't need your message, Mr. President, talk to the men.

This incident reiterates the observation I made at the start of this book—that rape is widely regarded as women's problem. Despite the fact that men are the perpetrators of sexual violence, it is women who continue to be perceived as responsible, either by causing rape or by failing to avoid it, and it is women who somehow are supposed to solve "their" problem. I have argued that this ideology, like sexual violence itself, is the result of the greater power of men to mold culture and define knowledge. In this tradition, the disease model of rape has been a force in maintaining the status quo by promulgating the view that sexual violence is a psychopathologically isolated, idiosyncratic act limited to a few "sick" men.

This vocabulary of denial was evident in the mass media reporting of the tragic December 6, 1989, massacre at the engineering school of the University of Montreal. A young man, armed with a semiautomatic assault rifle, murdered 14 women while shouting, "You are all a bunch of feminists. I hate feminists." Predictably, his actions were attributed to a disturbed psyche and the beatings his mother, sister, and he received from his father. The fact that his terror was directed at assumed feminists and that he was lucid enough to avoid classes, like nursing or social work, where women "belong," in favor of engineering, a male stronghold where women "don't belong," appears to have gone unnoticed. In fact, the politics of these murders—that this event, though extreme, is part of the general pattern of systematic sexual violence and the liability women collectively face—for the most part was ignored (see Caputi 1989).

In contrast to the psychopathological model, this book is grounded in a feminist perspective and the assumption that sexual violence is sociocultural in origin: men learn to rape. Thus, rather than examining the case histories of sexually violent men for evidence of pathology (in the traditional literature, often blamed on their mothers or wives) or for individual motives, I have used convicted rapists collectively as expert informants on a sexually violent culture. This approach generates questions and answers that are decidedly different from those contained in the nonfeminist literature. Rather than assuming that rape is dysfunctional for men, I asked instead what goals men have learned to achieve through sexually violent means.

Indeed, we find that men who rape do have something to tell us about the cultural roots of sexual violence. As they talk about what they gain from sexual violence, we are forced to acknowledge that rape is more than an idiosyncratic act committed by a few "sick" men. They tell us that some men use rape as a means of revenge and punishment. Implicit in revenge rape is the collective liability of women. In some cases, victims are substitutes for significant women on whom men desire to take revenge. In other cases, victims represent all women and rape is used to punish, humiliate, and "put them in their place." In either case women are seen as objects, a category, but not as individuals with rights. For some men, rape is an afterthought or a bonus they add to a burglary or a robbery. In other words, rape is "no big deal," just another part of the routine. Other men use sexual violence to gain access to unavailable or unwilling women—a tactic they use when a date says no. Some men rape in groups as a male bonding activity—for them, it's just something to do. For some men, rape is a fantasy come true, a particularly exciting form of impersonal sex that they enjoy because it enables them to dominate and control women by exercising a singularly male form of power. These men also talk of the pleasures of raping—how it is a challenge, an adventure, a dangerous and "ultimate" experience. Rape makes them feel good and, in some cases, elevates their self-image.

Thus, in the same way that motives for other acts can be rationally determined, reasons for rape can also be determined. Convicted rapists tell us that some men rape because they have learned that in this culture, sexual violence is rewarding. Significantly, almost no one in this sample thought he would go to prison for raping. In fact, these men perceived rape as a rewarding, low-risk act.

Types of Men Who Rape

But it is not enough to ask what motivates men to rape. We must also ask how rape is made possible in sexually violent cultures. The social constructions of reality of men who admit rape and of those who deny reveal the excuses and justifications that sustain sexual violence.

Admitters are one type of men who rape. They express the belief that rape is reprehensible and they understand women's fear of sexual violence. They explain themselves and their actions by appealing to forces beyond their control, forces that they say reduce their capacity to act rationally and thus compel them to rape. Two types of excuses predominate: minor emotional problems and drunkenness or disinhibition, which evidence suggests is also learned behavior. Admitters use these excuses to view their sexual violence as idiosyncratic rather than typical behavior. This allows them to conceptualize themselves as nice guys who made mistakes that do not represent their "true" selves.

But when they are raping, admitters are far from nice guys. They demonstrate that they are aware of the generalized image women have of rapists. Consistent with that knowledge, they perceive themselves to be violent and subhuman creatures, an image they use to their advantage—to terrify their victims and to render them subdued and compliant. Admitters also are aware of the emotional impact of rape on women, and they take satisfaction in the belief that their victims feel powerless, humiliated, and degraded—the way they want the women to feel. Thus, admitters are men who know what they are doing when they rape, who use their perceptiveness to enhance the satisfaction they experience from sexual violence, and who later use excuses to remove the blame.

In contrast, deniers, another type of sexually violent men, rape because their value system provides no compelling reason not to. These men use justifications to argue that their behavior, even if not quite right, is situationally appropriate. Their denials are drawn from common cultural rape stereotypes and take two forms, both of which ultimately deny the existence of victims.

The first form of denial is buttressed by the cultural view of men as sexually masterful and women as coy but seductive. Injury is denied by portraying the victim as willing, even enthusiastic, or as politely resistant at first but eventually yielding to "relax and enjoy it." Force is made to appear as merely a technique of seduction. Rape is disclaimed because, rather than harming the woman, they have made her dreams (nightmares) come true. In the second form of denial, the victim is portrayed as the type of woman who "got what she deserved." Through attacks on a woman's sexual reputation and her emotional state, these men argue that since the victim isn't "a nice girl," they are not rapists. Consistent with both forms of denial is the self-interested use of alcohol and drugs as an explanation. Thus, in contrast to admitters, who accentuate their own use as an excuse, deniers emphasize the victim's consumption in an effort both to discredit her and to make her appear more responsible while justifying their own behavior.

Deniers are characterized by a relative absence of self-awareness. They either do not care how their victims perceive them or believe their victims would describe them as kind, gentle, and desirable, or as good lovers. Deniers also either are unaware of their victims' feelings or, consistent with cultural stereotypes, assume that once the rape begins, victims will relax and enjoy it. Deniers, then, represent the type of men who lack self-awareness and who are so imperceptive they are incapable of understanding the meaning of sexual violence to women.

"Pedestal" Values and Other Dangerous Attitudes

Admitters and deniers present a contrast in the types of men who rape. Yet, despite the differences, they are the same in one essential way. The majority do not experience guilt or shame as a result of raping, nor do they report feeling any emotions for their victims during or following the rape. Instead of experiencing feelings that might constrain their sexually violent behavior, these men indicate that rape causes them to feel nothing or to feel good. To understand the absence of emotions, it is necessary to examine the perspective of these men toward women in general and toward their victims in particular.

Members of a shared culture can be expected to have somewhat similar attitudes, but sexually violent men are more extreme in their beliefs. They are characterized by an intensely rigid double standard of moral and sexual conduct—a standard that both denies a woman the rights accorded to men and requires her to have the protection of a man. These "pedestal" values, far from reflecting positive feelings for women, as myth would have us believe, spring from intolerance and are associated with very hostile and violent attitudes toward women. Sexually violent men identify with traditional images of masculinity and male gender role privilege; they believe very strongly in rape stereotypes, and for them, being male carries the right to discipline and punish women.

Men are able to rape because their victims have no real or symbolic meaning or value outside of the role rapists force them to perform. The satisfaction such men derive from sexual violence reveals the extreme to which our culture has enabled them to objectify women. Women are jokes, objects, targets, sexual commodities, pieces of property to be used or conquered, not human beings with rights and feelings. Since actions directed at meaningless objects do not evoke feelings, emotions fail to constrain their sexually violent behavior. Hierarchical gender relations and the corresponding values that devalue women and diminish them to exploitable objects or property are the factors that render feeling rules inoperative and empower men to rape. One young man expressed the extreme of this contempt for women when he confided to me:

> Rape is a man's right. If a woman doesn't want to give it, a man should take it. Women have no right to say no. Women are made to have sex. It's all they are good for. Some women would rather take a beating, but they always give in; it's what they are for.

This man murdered his victim when she wouldn't "give in."

Patriarchy and the Inevitability of Sexual Violence

If sexual violence and all its manifestations are the inevitable consequence of patriarchal social structure, as feminist theory argues, it is clear that prison alone is not the solution to eliminating the vast amount of violence directed at women. How many prisons would it take to contain all men who are sexually violent? Only profound social change at both the micro and macro levels of society is capable of eroding the rape-supportive elements of our culture. For starters, we must refuse to accept the excuses and justifications that are used to trivialize and neutralize rape, and that sustain a cultural environment in which sexual violence is acceptable to and rewarding for men. The factors that abridge women's rights as full human beings and the barriers that prevent women from acting in accordance with those rights and achieving full parity with men must be removed. We must acknowledge that the origins of violence in the family are to be found in the structural subordination of women, and thus this violence is a symptom, not the cause, of the larger social problem. Among other things, this means treating crimes against women—including assaults by family members, husbands, lovers, friends, bosses, and acquaintances—with the same degree of severity as crimes against men and against strangers. When this happens, women will feel safer in reporting all those crimes against them that now go unnoticed. We must stop accepting psychiatric and other vocabularies of motive that enable men to avoid responsibility for their sexually violent behavior. We must stop blaming sexual violence on race, class, alcohol, and drugs, and, even though it is threatening, we must accept that sexually violent men are otherwise normal and that, for some men, sex is rape. And we must understand the power of those who define knowledge and be ever vigilant, because just as one ideology of denial begins its demise, another comes along—witness the newest vocabulary of motive for rape, this time the contribution of sociobiologists.

Starting with Thornhill and Thornhill's (1983) questionable observation that forced copulation appears to occur among scorpionflies, some sociobiologists have advanced an evolutionary explanation for rape.[1] Bouncing from insect behavior to human behavior in advanced industrialized societies, some sociobiologists claim that rape is one of several adaptive reproductive strategies used by males to ensure their "inclusive fitness," measured by success in passing genes along to future generations of progeny. While agreeing in principle on the definition of rape as an "evolved facultative behavior", proponents disagree over who rapes and which "forced copulations" are to be considered rape. Shields and Shields (1983, 123) argue that all men are potential rapists because, "during human evolutionary history, males that possessed a mating strategy that included rape as a facultative response were favored by natural selection over those that did not." Thornhill and Thornhill (1983) disagree, arguing that high-status men rarely rape and, even when they do force copulation, it is not really rape because of the implicit benefit to the woman. They state:

167

Copulation by a man with women who depend on him or are under his control (e.g., a male employer copulating with his female secretary or a male slaveowner with his female slave) is not *necessarily* rape (or any other form of sexual conflict) by our definition because the female need not be denied the option of gaining benefits that exceed costs to reproduction [job security or salary (secretary); resources or higher status for self or offspring (slave)]. We are not saying that men in powerful positions never rape women dependent upon them. But we limit actual rape in such circumstances to situations in which a copulation is forced in the sense that the female loses her ability to use copulation in her own reproductive interest. (p. 141)

The masculinity of science is evident in the work of these scientists, who not only impose their untested speculations on sexual violence, but claim the right to determine who rapes and what acts are to be considered rape based not on women's experience of violation or even on the facts of the case, but on the social status and power of the perpetrator!

Finally, men must take responsibility for sexual violence and work collectively to change those aspects of male culture that support the abuse of women. Apropos of this observation, a recent popular talk show featured as its theme "men who have been harmed by rape." All of the guests were fathers, husbands, or brothers of women who had been raped, and they talked passionately about the anguish it had caused them, how it had changed their lives. Predictably, they also expressed anger and the desire for revenge, and they talked about the need to protect their daughters, wives, and sisters.

I was struck by the similarity between the reactions of these men, sincere as they were, and the response of convicted rapists when I asked them how they would feel and what they would do if their own significant women were raped. The overwhelming reaction among rapists, 72 percent of admitters and 75 percent of deniers, was an expression of anger and violence. Additionally, the majority of these men said that rather than involving law enforcement, they would find a way to get personal revenge. Many of them simply answered, "I would find the guy and kill him," and a few reflected that their victims' men should have done the same to them. Since men who rape also abuse, rape, and are violent toward their own significant women, this reaction hardly expresses care or the desire to protect "their" women for the women's own sakes. For example, speaking for a number of the men, one rapist stated:

> If I felt she was at fault or gave a come on, I would say she got what she deserved. If I thought the guy was at fault, I'd blow his goddamn brains out. And if she was my old lady and she was responsible, I'd blow hers out too.

Unfortunately, this type of male reaction to rape appears common, and it is part of the problem. It is a reflection of traditional attitudes and values that mandate violence and revenge when a man's own property is violated by another man because he, not the woman, is the offended party. In the final analysis, women's interests are not served by individual efforts to protect some women or by acts of revenge, but only by efforts to eliminate sexual violence toward all women.

Women have not been passive recipients of sexual violence. We have organized, protested, fought, counseled, cried together, marched, debunked myths, tried to "take back the night," challenged authority, learned self-defense, operated hot lines, changed laws, raised money, built shelters, written voluminously—everything but commit acts of violence. Yet I believe that no fundamental change will occur until men are forced to admit that sexual violence is *their* problem. I hope that, in some modest way, this book will contribute to that end.

Note

1 For a critique of the research on rape among animals and the evolutionary perspective on rape, see Fausto-Sterling (1985 chap. 6).

Afterword:
Defending Against Rape

My focus in this book has been on understanding sexual violence as men's problem, but the reality is that women are the ones at risk. Thus, I conclude with this afterword on defending against rape. This is not intended to be an exhaustive analysis of rape avoidance strategies; rather, it is offered in the hope that something useful can be learned from the source of the problem, convicted rapists themselves—they are, after all, the real experts.

Fear of Rape

Research consistently demonstrates what women already know—fear of rape is widespread. In a survey of urban women and men, Warr (1985) found that fear of rape is extremely high among women of all ages, and, among women under the age of 35, rape is feared more than any other crime, including murder, assault, and robbery. Conceptualizing fear as the product of two related factors, perceived seriousness and feelings of personal risk, Warr found that rape is an exception to the general pattern, in which the more serious the crime, the less women expect to be victimized by it. In the case of rape, fear is related to the seriousness of the crime and the fact that women view it as relatively likely to happen to them. Fear of being murdered contributes to fear of rape. Stanko (1985), for example, found that part of women's fear is the perceived possibility of being killed or mutilated during a rape.

It is not clear from Warr's questionnaire, but several observations make it appear that it is the "classic" rape by a stranger on the street that women fear most. For example, assault by a stranger is perceived as more serious and more likely to happen, and is more feared by the women he surveyed than assault by someone known. In contrast, these women regard an assault by someone known as less serious and less likely to occur, and, consequently, they have relatively little fear of this type of crime. Precautionary behavior also reflects perceived differences in risk. In Warr's survey, the majority of precautions consist of life-style restrictions and security outside of the home, for example, avoiding certain areas of the city, going out alone, going out at night, or answering the door. A sizable proportion of the women surveyed by Riger and Gordon (1981) also used isolation tactics on a regular basis. Indeed, all the bars I see on women's windows represent to me the hallmark of a sexually violent society, in which it is the victims who are the ones in prison.

These patterns in women's fear are understandable within the context of societal stereotypes about who and what sexually violent men are. Street crime is terrifying, and it is a risk that women do face. However, data suggest that the men women know pose a risk at least as great as strangers of assault or rape and serious injury, including murder, which rarely occurs within the context of stranger rapes. And because the family is the locus of much violence and murder, the homes of many women are far from safe havens. Nonetheless, the research of Riger and Gordon and Warr demonstrates the far-reaching effects of sexual violence in this society. Women fear rape and assault by strangers, and they adjust their life-styles accordingly. Thus, as Warr points out, the social consequence of rape is not limited to those women who have been directly victimized by it. In fact, fear of rape restricts women's life-styles in ways that fear of crime does not restrict men. For example, among the men in Warr's survey, very few indicated a curtailment of life-style as a result of risk of crime. In fact, this research shows the dramatic social control function that rape has over women in sexually violent societies—a function, feminists argue, that operates to the benefit of *all* men, whether sexually violent or not.

What Would a Rapist Do?

Strategies for successfully avoiding rape have been examined in several studies, including analysis of National Crime Survey data by Griffin and Griffin (1981) and by Lizotte (1986), analysis of Canadian offenders' records by Quinsey and Upfold (1985), and interview research by Bart and O'Brien (1984, 1985) in which the tactics used by women who avoided rape were compared to the tactics of women who were the victims of completed rapes. In general, this research has shown that women who resist physically have a better chance of avoiding rape than those who do not. Until the study reported here, however, men who rape had not been asked for their opinions, so I asked them. Convicted rapists were questioned about a number of factors relevant to rape avoidance, including how they chose their victims, what their original intent had been, when the decision to rape was made, how they gained compliance, how their victims reacted, how they thought they would have reacted to similar attacks, and what they thought their victims could have done to avoid being raped without being injured.

A number of caveats apply to this discussion, and they are important to understand. First, deniers' social construction of reality makes them unsuitable informants on rape avoidance; consequently, I have examined only the rapes committed by 46 admitters. For purposes of analysis, the rapes are divided into stranger, 36 cases, and acquaintance, 10 cases, and further categorized by number of assailants, injury to victim, and presence of a weapon. Thus, not only is the sample small, but the discussion of some types of rape is based on very few cases and may not be representative of the type at all. Additionally, it is important to keep in mind that although admitters were generally sincere in their desire to contribute helpful information, like deniers (albeit to a lesser degree), they understated the amount of violence they used, the presence and role of weapons, and the amount of injury to their victims. In every case, these facts were carefully checked against their records for accuracy, but, unfortunately, the information was not always complete. With these limitations in mind, the purpose here is to analyze the crimes, rather than the men who committed them, with the hope that women will feel less need to restrict their life-styles and better prepared to defend themselves in potential rape encounters.

Stranger Rapes

Among admitters, the largest number of cases was 26 stranger rapes involving a lone assailant. The majority occurred at night and were street crimes. In fact, predictable in a prison sample, they were the classic "noncontroversial" rape, which is also the crime that women appear to fear most.

From a woman's perspective, this type of rape is sudden and terrifying and the unexpectedness of the attack produces a tactical disadvantage. But what about the perpetrator? Is this type of rape more likely to have been a sudden, spontaneous act, or one that was planned? In response to questions about their original intent and when the decision to rape was made, the majority of these men, 58 percent, indicated that their original intent had been to rape; 27 percent intended to rob or burglarize the victim, and the remainder intended something else, such as repairing the victim's stalled car. In almost every case in which the original intent had been to rape, it also had been planned. That is, far from spontaneous, the men indicated they had been thinking about raping for hours or, in some cases, several days before acting. In most cases, they went out on the night of the rape with a plan, looking for a victim, and with the specific intent to rape. In those cases where the original intent had been to rob or burglarize, the decision to rape was made after a sense of control over the situation was established. Elsewhere, I have referred to these rapes as "an added bonus" because the attitude expressed by the men was, if the situation is right, "why not?"

Like any woman, I was particularly interested in learning how victims are chosen in stranger rapes. Is it something about the woman or her appearance or her behavior that selects her for victimization? The answer is unequivocally no. In every case except possibly one hitchhiking-related rape, women were conducting the ordinary business of their daily lives. They were at home or work, but more often they were going to or from home, work, stores, or school. In the majority of cases they were walking, were in a parking lot, or were in a stranded car when approached. Six women were attacked in their homes and one in her office. But the most striking and consistent factor in all the stranger rapes, whether committed by a lone assailant or a group, is the unfortunate fact that the victim was "just there" in a location unlikely to draw the attention of a passerby. Almost every one of these men said exactly the same thing, "It could have been any woman," and a few added that because it was dark, they could not even see what their victim looked like very well. Said one typical man, "Didn't have to be her, she was just there at the wrong time." In those cases where the victim was attacked in her home, the house or apartment was selected, not the victim, because it appeared relatively easy and safe for breaking and entering and the victim looked "helpless," for example, asleep. Thus, the answer to women who have wondered "Why me?" is simple—randomness and convenience. For sexually violent men, women are interchangeable objects and one is as good as any other.

The tactics used to gain initial compliance and whether or not a weapon is present are important in deciding how to respond in an attack. Although their records were sometimes unclear, it appears that in 62 percent of these rapes a weapon was present, most frequently a knife, and in an additional two cases, a weapon was faked. To gain compliance, the men used a combination of terror tactics, including sudden attack in dark and/or deserted places (or where they were least likely to draw attention), showing weapons along with verbal threats of mutilation and/or death (the threat that women fear most), and physical force such as restraining, knocking down, choking, and hitting with fists and/or weapons. However, in the majority of cases, the weapon was used primarily to terrorize and subdue the victim, but not to inflict serious injury. Likewise, Griffin and Griffin (1981) conclude that the majority of women confronted with weapon threats do not sustain serious injury, although it is not clear whether this can be explained by lack of victim resistance, and Quinsey and Upfold (1985) found that, unlike in acquaintance rapes, in stranger rapes injury is associated with the absence of a weapon. While sometimes difficult to determine from the records, it appears that 17 of the 26 admitters' victims escaped with minor injuries beyond the rape, such as shallow cuts, bruises, scratches, and torn clothing. In an attempt to discover factors related to injury in rape, it is necessary to make a distinction between serious and minor injury, keeping in mind that all of the rapes were brutal.

Admitters were men who understood the meaning of rape to women, and they both perceived and enjoyed the fear they evoked in their victims. They expected, and from their perspective for the most part got, compliant victims. Several women were reported to have screamed and/or struggled, fewer to have tried to talk their way out, but, according to these men, the majority submitted and many cried. For example, one rapist expressed being surprised by one of his multiple victims because, unlike the others, she fought, and hard. Several points are relevant here. First, the meaning of *fight* to sexually violent men may require the use of considerably more aggression than it does for women. Second, if women who resist physically are more likely to avoid being raped, the fact that these are completed rapes may explain the relatively large proportion of women who did not physically resist. But the issue is, are women who resist more likely to be injured?

Keeping in mind the limitations of this sample, that the number of rapes being analyzed is small, and that I am relying on less than complete data and on the perceptions of sexually violent men, the answer is a cautious no. In this sample, resistance, defined as screaming or fighting, did not result in more injury than talking or doing nothing. Roughly the same proportion of women who resisted and women who did not were seriously injured. In the two cases that culminated in murder, one victim fought, and, while the reaction of the other victim is not clear, since her attacker was a serial murderer-rapist who planned all of his murder-rapes, fighting could not have resulted in greater injury.

Among men who did not inflict serious injury, the majority, 10 out of the 17, said that if their victims had run, screamed, or fought, they could have avoided rape; 4 men specifically indicated they would not have used their weapons. Said one attacker, "If she had screamed or fought back it might have worked. The whimpering just didn't work enough." A minority, 3 men, advocated talking, but 4 men indicated there was essentially nothing their victims could have done to avoid rape without injury, and, if they had resisted, they might have been injured. For example, "If she had used physical resistance I might have hurt her because I'm geared to protecting myself." Of the 7 men who did injure their victims, 4 said there was nothing the victims could have done, and the remainder thought the victims could have screamed or run. Men who had weapons, whether or not they used them to injure their victims, were more likely to say there was nothing their victims could have done, and, in both cases of murder, there was nothing the victims could have done, according to their assailants.

Interestingly, when asked what they would have done in their victims' place, a modest majority, 55 percent, responded run, scream, or fight; 35 percent responded they would have done what their victims did, submit; and the remainder said they would have tried to talk their way out. Men who possessed weapons and those who did not were equally likely to advocate resistance, as were men who inflicted serious injury and those who did not. Those who said they would have submitted considered the situation too dangerous to resist, and several men mentioned how angry they had been, suggesting that they feel resistance would have resulted in getting hurt. A few men understood the limitations of traditional female socialization, which teaches women to be passive and "ladylike," and, putting themselves in their victims' place, decided they would not have been aggressive. For example, "Hard to say, I'm a man and can't strip myself of self-defense knowledge. I wasn't brought up to be helpless. Probably same as her [submit]."

Group Rapes

Group rapes, defined as involving two or more men, compound the danger to the victim. Not only must she face multiple assailants, but the driving force in these rapes—"macho," male camaraderie, adventure, and "proving" yourself capable in front of others—means that each assailant has a particular vested interest in completing the rape. Among admitters, there were ten group rapes, and they had a number of characteristics in common with rapes involving a lone assailant. All of them involved strangers and, with the exception of one hitchhiking rape, all were street abductions of women as they carried out routine activities. (All of the "gang date" rapes discussed in Chapter 6 were committed by deniers, who, because they said they knew "it was the kind of thing she liked," did not define what they did as rape.) With one exception, all the rapes occurred at night. Of these rapes, two women were murdered, three women were seriously injured, and five women escaped injury. As with other stranger rapes, in every case the victim was randomly abducted because "she was just there." In the majority of cases, rape had been the original intent and it had been planned. In half the rapes, weapons were used to terrify the victims and, in several cases, both guns and knives had been present. Faced by more than one man and a small arsenal of weapons, the majority of these women did not physically resist their attackers. As with other stranger rapes, advice on what the victim could have done was mixed. In the rapes that did not culminate in murder, three of the men indicated that there was nothing the victims could have done to avoid the rapes without being more seriously injured, but the majority said she could have run, screamed, or fought. Likewise, all but two of these men said they would have fought or screamed. In the two group murders—rapes, both men said there was nothing the victim could have done and that they also would have submitted, to get it over with quickly.

Acquaintance Rapes

Relatively few rapes among admitters involved acquaintances, for several reasons. Compared to rapes involving strangers, women are less likely to report rapes that involve men they know, and, when they do report an acquaintance rape, they are less likely to be believed. Acquaintance rapists are less likely to be prosecuted and, if prosecuted, are less likely to be convicted. Therefore, acquaintance rapes are underrepresented in prison populations. Additionally, this research suggests that men who rape acquaintances, even if they are convicted, are more likely to deny that what they did was rape than are men who rape strangers. The result is a larger proportion of acquaintance rapes among deniers than among admitters.

There were ten acquaintance rapes among admitters, and each involved a lone assailant. The characteristics of these rapes are quite different from stranger rapes. The majority occurred at night in the victims' homes, where the man had gained entrance legitimately. Victims were not selected randomly because they were "just there"; in almost every case, the man expressed a previous sexual attraction for the victim, who did not return his interest. Compared to the planning in stranger rapes, acquaintance rapes were somewhat more spontaneous. That is, in the majority of cases, the men did not go to the victims' homes with the specific intent to rape. However, the reason for the men's being there was related to their sexual interests. Thus, the original intent had been something else, and when the women refused sex, the men decided to use force.

Acquaintance rapes were far from gentle seductions. In about a third of these rapes, weapons had been present; in a few cases, a knife from the victim's kitchen was used. The tactics used to create fear and gain compliance were the same as in stranger rapes—verbal threats with and without a weapon, restraining, beating, and choking. Half the victims suffered serious injury, and, in one case, death, because according to her murderer, "I told her 'I'll get it one way or another' and I did." As with the stranger rapes, it is not possible to determine accurately how these women reacted to the attacks. According to the records, it appears most did struggle. According to their rapists, however, for the most part they submitted, which some of the men said they interpreted as consent. Had they been in their victims' situation, the majority of these men would have fought. However, when asked what their victims could have done, only two men responded fight, several advocated talking, and the remainder said there was nothing the victims could have done.

Defending Against Rape

I have spent ten years doing research and writing about sexually violent men, yet I stop here, short of giving advice. It may be helpful to keep in mind that even in the crime that women fear most, street rape by a stranger, most incidents do not result in serious physical injury to the victim, even when a weapon is used to threaten, and the vast majority of men who rape strangers do not murder their victims. These men are dangerous, however, and the exact amount of risk to the victim is never certain. Some men are very angry and are using their victims for revenge; many are experienced rapists, and, more than likely, they have planned the rape. They expect a predictable response from their victims—pleading, fear, passivity—because this behavior allows them to control.

Nonetheless, all the recent research finds that women who resist have a better chance of avoiding rape (Griffin and Griffin 1981; Lizotte 1986; Quinsey and Upfold 1985). In their comparison of women who avoided and those who did not, Bart and O'Brien (1985) found not only that avoiders used more strategies but they also used strategies different from those used by women who were raped. Women who avoided were more likely to flee or try to flee, to talk loudly or scream, to use physical force, and to be aided by environmental intervention. Raped women were more likely to plead, and both groups used cognitive verbal skills. Not only is pleading ineffective, it may even have unintended consequences. It is worth noting that several men specifically quoted their victims as saying, "I'll do anything, just don't hurt me," which indicated to them they were in control and able to carry out a rape. The lesson is, don't offer! Confirming the wisdom of avoiders, the majority of men who raped strangers also indicated that their victims could have avoided being raped by using a combination of essentially the same strategies listed above. For the most part, these are the strategies rapists themselves said they would have used if they had been in their victims' situation. Western culture has produced men who are preoccupied with predictability and order and disconcerted by chaos and irregularity because, whether in science, business, or rape, it is less controllable. Keep in

180

mind that for men, a major function of sexual violence is the domination and control of women.

Fear of serious injury, mutilation, and death prevents many women from resisting potential attackers. However, recent research evidence suggests that active resistance is not strongly related to serious physical injury and that passive resistance—such as pleading—does not guarantee a lack of injury. Among the victims of the rapists in this research, women who physically resisted were not more seriously injured than women who did not resist physically. And Bart and O'Brien (1985) conclude that women who resist physically are more likely to avoid rape but often do sustain minor injuries such as scratches and bruises. This observation is reinforced by the majority of men who raped strangers and who said that they would not have seriously injured their victims if they had attempted to resist physically. On the other hand, several men said they would have. The problem is, how to judge.

Research that has attempted to answer this question by untangling any observed correlation between victim resistance and serious physical injury has concluded that the relationship is a spurious one. Griffin and Griffin (1981) argue that injury increases relative to the seriousness of the initial threat, not victim resistance. In their work with National Crime Survey data they found that serious injury is most likely to occur in those rapes where an immediate physical threat is used. Quinsey and Upfold (1985) have attempted to answer this question by examining the sequencing of events in the rapes they studied. Their data show that the positive relationship between victim resistance and injury is a result of the fact that victims resisted more strongly *when* they were being injured. There was no association between victim resistance and the probability of *later* injury. In fact, any resistance with an unknown assailant was associated with a lower probability of injury.

Resisting an attack that occurs in the home may present more obstacles than street rape, but even these assaults can be successfully avoided. While I was working on this chapter, an attempted rape occurred in the duplex next to mine. It was a warm August night at about 11:00 p.m., when I heard

181

loud pounding, sounds of physical struggle, and a woman screaming "Rape!" through our adjoining walls. After calling the emergency number, I, along with a number of other neighbors, converged on her locked front door and started pounding. This distracted her would-be attacker and she was able to escape through the back door. She was very smart, very brave, and she did everything right. She had been in the rear of the apartment when she heard noises coming from the front (he broke in through a front window that was locked open at about a foot) and immediately picked up the phone and called a friend who lives on the street. Before her friend could arrive, her assailant grabbed her and the attempted rape began. She used a combination of every avoidance strategy known to be successful. She alerted a friend, screamed, made noise, physically resisted, and ran, and she escaped without physical injury. Her neighbors helped, too, by responding to her screams for help and by attempting to intervene.

While women may have less fear of the men they know, this research demonstrates that rape by acquaintances can be just as brutal as rape involving a stranger. Clearly, knowing a man does not necessarily make him less dangerous. For example, Quinsey and Upfold (1985) found that assailants were more likely to complete rapes when the attacks occurred indoors, with weapons, and against victims they knew. Additionally, victims known to assailants were more likely to be injured than were strangers (although this may be the result of using a prison sample). In general, the same strategies used to avoid a stranger can be used to defend against an acquaintance, date, husband, or lover. Even better, when possible, it is wise to avoid the type of sexually violent men described in this book.

As I complete this afterword, I am aware that it is less than satisfying. But, in the final analysis, what to do and how much risk to take when confronted by a threatening situation is each woman's individual choice. And no woman should ever be blamed or made to feel responsible for not avoiding a rape. I do believe, however, that knowledge is power. I hope that, armed with an understanding of the men and the crime, women will have a greater advantage!

Bibliography

Abel, G. G., D. H. Barlow, E. B. Blanchard, and D. Guild (1977). "The Components of Rapists' Sexual Arousal." *Archives of General Psychology*, 34, 895–908.

Abel, G. G., J. V. Becker, E. B. Blanchard, and A. Djenderedjian (1978). "Differentiating Sexual Aggressives with Penile Measures." *Criminal Justice and Behavior*, 5, 315–22.

Abel, G. G., J. V. Becker, and L. J. Skinner (1980). "Aggressive Behavior and Sex." *Psychiatric Clinics of North America*, 3, 133—51.

Abel, G. G., E. B. Blanchard, D. H. Barlow, and M. Mavissakalian (1975). "Identifying Specific Erotic Cues in Sexual Deviations by Audio-taped Descriptions: A Preliminary Report." *Journal of Applied Behavioral Analysis*, 8, 247–60.

Abrahamsen, David (1960). *The Psychology of Crime*. New York: John Wiley.

Acock, A., and N. Ireland (1981). "Attribution of Blame in Rape Cases: The Impact of Norm Violation, Gender, and Sex Role Attitude." Paper presented at the annual meetings of the American Sociological Association.

Albin, Rochelle (1977). "Psychological Studies of Rape." *Signs*, 3, 23–35.

Amir, Menachem (1971). *Patterns in Forcible Rape*. Chicago: University of Chicago Press.

——— (1972). "The Role of the Victim in Sex Offenses." In H. Resnik and M. Wolfgang, eds., *Sexual Behavior: Social, Clinical, and Legal Aspects*. Boston: Little, Brown.

Athens, Lonnie (1977). "Violent Crime: A Symbolic Interactionist Study." *Symbolic Interaction*, 1, 56–71.

Attorney General's Commission on Pornography (July, 1986). *Final Report*, 2 vols. Washington, DC: Government Printing Office.

Barbaree, H. E., W. L. Marshall, and R. D. Lanthier (1979). "Deviant Sexual Arousal in Rapists." *Behavioral Research and Therapy*, 17, 215–22.

Bart, Pauline B., (1979). "Rape as a Paradigm of Sexism in Society—

Victimization and Its Discontents." *Women's Studies International Quarterly*, 2, 347–57.

Bart, Pauline B., and M. Jozsa (1980). "Dirty Books, Dirty Films and Dirty Data." In L. Lederer, ed., *Take Back the Night: Women on Pornography*. New York: William Morrow.

Bart, Pauline B., and Patricia H. O'Brien (1984). "Stopping Rape: Effective Avoidance Strategies." *Signs*, 10, 83–101.

———— (1985). *Stopping Rape: Successful Survival Strategies*. New York: Pergamon.

Bender, L. (1965). "Offended and Offender Children." In R. Slovenko, ed., *Sexual Behavior and the Law*. Springfield, IL: Charles C Thomas.

Ben-Veniste, R. (1971). "Pornography and Sex Crime: The Danish Experience." In *Technical Reports of the Commission on Obscenity and Pornography*, Vol. 8. Washington, DC: Government Printing Office.

Black, Donald (1983). "Crime as Social Control." *American Sociological Review*, 48, 34–45.

Bleier, Ruth (1984). *Science and Gender: A Critique of Biology and Its Theories on Women*. New York: Pergamon.

Blumberg, Rae Lesser (1979). "A Paradigm for Predicting the Position of Women: Policy Implications and Problems." In Jean Lipman-Blumen and Jessie Bernard, eds., *Sex Roles and Social Policy*. London: Sage.

Borgida, E., and P. White (1979). "Judgmental Bias and Legal Reform." Unpublished manuscript, University of Minnesota.

Bowman, K., and B. Engle (1965). "Sexual Psychopath Laws." In R. Slovenko, ed., *Sexual Behavior and the Law*. Springfield, IL: Charles C Thomas.

Bradburn, N., and S. Sudman (1979). *Improving Interview Method and Questionnaire Design*. San Francisco: Jossey-Bass.

Brain, Paul F., ed. (1986). *Alcohol and Aggression*. London: Croom Helm.

Brannon, Robert (1976). "The Male Sex Role: Our Culture's Blueprint of Manhood and What It's Done for Us Lately." In Deborah David and Robert Brannon, eds., *The Forty-Nine Percent Majority: The Male Sex Role*. Reading, MA: Addison-Wesley.

Brent, Linda (1973). *Incidents in the Life of a Slave Girl*. San Diego: Harcourt Brace Jovanovich. (reprint)

Briere, John, and Neil Malamuth (1983). "Self-Reported Likelihood of Sexually Aggressive Behavior: Attitudinal Versus Sexual Explanations." *Journal of Research in Personality*, 17, 315–23.

Brod, Harry, ed. (1986). *The Making of Masculinities: The New Men's Studies*. Boston: Allen & Unwin.

Broude, Gwen, and Sarah Greene (1976). "Cross-Cultural Codes on Twenty Sexual Attitudes and Practices." *Ethnology*, 15, 409–28.

Brownmiller, Susan (1975). *Against Our Will: Men, Women and Rape*. New York: Simon & Schuster.

Burgess, Ann Wolbert, and Lynda Lytle Holmstrom (1979). "Rape: Sexual Disruption and Recovery." *American Journal of Orthopsychiatry*, 49, 648–57.

———— (1974). *Rape: Victims of Crisis*. Bowie, MD: Robert J. Brady.

Burt, Martha (1978). "Antecedents of Rape Myth Acceptance and Consequences for Apprehending and Treating Assailants." Paper presented at the annual meetings of the American Psychological Association.

———— (1980). "Cultural Myths and Supports for Rape." *Journal of Personality and Social Psychology*, 38, 217–30.

Burt, Martha, and Rochelle Albin (1981). "Rape Myths, Rape Definitions, and Probability of Conviction." *Journal of Applied Social Psychology*, 11, 212–30.

Calhoun, L. (1978). "The Effect of Victim Physical Attractiveness and Sex of Respondent on Social Reaction to Victims of Rape." *British Journal of Clinical Psychology*, 17, 191–92.

Calhoun, L., J. Selby, and L. Warring (1976). "Social Perception of the Victim's Causal Role in Rape: An Exploratory Examination of Four Factors." *Human Relations*, 29, 517–26.

Caputi, Jane (1989). "The Sexual Politics of Murder." *Gender and Society*, 3, 437–56.

Carpenter, John A., and Nicholas P. Armenti (1972). "Some Effects of Ethanol on Human Sexual and Aggressive Behavior." In B. Hessin and H. Begleiter, eds., *The Biology of Alcoholism*, Vol. 2. New York: Plenum.

Chancer, Lynn S. (1987). "New Bedford, Massachusetts, March 6, 1983–March 22, 1984: The 'Before and After' of a Group Rape." *Gender and Society*, 1, 239–60.

Chesler, Phyllis (1972). *Women and Madness*. Garden City, NY: Doubleday.

———— (1978). *About Men*. New York: Simon & Schuster.

Cicone, M., and D. Ruble (1978). "Beliefs About Males." *Journal of Social Issues*, 34, 5–16.

Clark, Lorenne, and Debra Lewis (1977). *Rape: The Price of Coercive Sexuality*. Toronto: Women's Press.

Coid, Jeremy (1986). "Alcohol, Rape and Sexual Assault." In P. F. Brain, ed., *Alcohol and Aggression*. London: Croom Helm.

Coleman, Diane H., and Murray A. Straus (1983). "Alcohol Abuse and Family Violence." In Edward Gottheil, Keith A. Druley, Thomas E. Skoloda, and Howard M. Waxman, eds., *Alcohol, Drug Abuse and Aggression*. Springfield, IL: Charles C Thomas.

Committee on Psychiatry and Law (1977). *Psychiatry and Sex Psychopath Legislation: The 30s to the 80s*. (Publication No. 98). New York: Group for the Advancement of Psychiatry.

Conrad, Peter, and Joseph W. Schneider, eds. (1980). *Deviance and Medicalization: From Badness to Sickness*. St. Louis: C. V. Mosby.

Cooley, Charles Horton (1902). *Human Nature and the Social Order*. New York: Scribner.

185

Court, John H. (1984). "Sex and Violence: A Ripple Effect." In Neil M. Malamuth and Edward Donnerstein, eds., *Pornography and Sexual Aggression*. New York: Academic Press.

Cowden, J., and A. Pacht (1969). "The Sex Inventory as a Classification Instrument for Sex Offenders." *Journal of Clinical Psychology*, 25, 53–57.

Davis, Angela (1981). *Women, Race and Class*. New York: Random House.

Dietz, P. (1978). "Social Factors in Rapists' Behavior." In Richard Rada, ed., *Clinical Aspects of the Rapist*. New York: Grune & Stratton.

Donnerstein, Edward (1980). "Aggressive Erotica and Violence Against Women." *Journal of Personality and Social Psychology*, 39, 269–77.

Donnerstein, Edward, and Gary Barrett (1978). "Effects of Erotic Stimuli on Male Aggression Toward Women." *Journal of Personality and Social Psychology*, 36, 180–88.

Donnerstein, Edward, Marcia Donnerstein, and Ronald Evans (1975). "Erotic Stimuli and Aggression: Facilitation or Inhibition." *Journal of Personality and Social Psychology*, 32, 237–44.

Donnerstein, Edward, and John Hallam (1978). "Facilitating Effects of Erotica on Aggression Towards Women." *Journal of Personality and Social Psychology*, 36, 1270–77.

Doyle, James A. (1983). *The Male Experience*. Dubuque, IA: Wm. C. Brown.

Dworkin, Andrea (1980). "The Prophet of Perversion." *Mother Jones*, April 24.

Edwards, Anne (1987). "Male Violence in Feminist Theory: An Analysis of the Changing Conceptions of Sex/Gender Violence and Male Domination." In Jalna Hanmer and Mary Maynard, eds., *Women, Violence and Social Control*. Atlantic Highlands, NJ: Humanities Press International.

Ellis, A., and R. Brancale (1956). *The Psychology of Sex Offenders*. Springfield, IL: Charles C Thomas.

Fausto-Sterling, Anne (1985). *Myths of Gender*. New York: Basic Books.

Federal Bureau of Investigation (1972). *Uniform Crime Reports*. Washington, DC: Government Printing Office.

Feild, H. (1978). "Attitudes Toward Rape: A Comparative Analysis of Police, Rapists, Crisis Counselors, and Citizens." *Journal of Personality and Social Psychology*, 35, 156–79.

Feldman-Sommers, Shirley, Patricia E. Gordon, and Jeanette R. Meagher (1979). "The Impact of Rape on Sexual Satisfaction." *Journal of Abnormal Psychology*, 88, 101–5.

Fine, Gary Allen (1986). *With the Boys*. Chicago: University of Chicago Press.

Finkelhor, David (1985). "Sexual Abuse of Boys." In Ann Wolbert Burgess, ed., *Rape and Sexual Assault: A Research Handbook*. New York: Garland.

Fisher, G., and E. Rivlin (1971). "Psychological Needs of Rapists." *British Journal of Criminology*, 11, 182–85.

Franks, David D. (1986). "Role-Taking, Social Power and Imperceptiveness: The Analysis of Rape." *Studies in Symbolic Interaction*, 6, 229–59.

Garfinkle, Harold (1956). "Conditions of a Successful Degradation Ceremony." *American Journal of Sociology*, 61, 420–24.

Gilligan, Carol (1982). *In a Different Voice: Psychological Theory and Women's Development*. Cambridge, MA: Harvard University Press.

Gilmartin-Zena, Pat (1988). "Gender Differences in Students' Attitudes Toward Rape." *Sociological Focus*, 21, 279–92.

Gollin, Albert E. (1980). "Comment on Johnson's 'On the Prevalence of Rape in the United States.' " *Signs*, 6, 346–49.

Griffin, Brenda S., and Charles T. Griffin (1981). "Victims in Rape Confrontation." *Victimology: An International Journal*, 6, 59–75.

Griffin, Susan (1971). "Rape: The All American Crime." *Ramparts*, September 10, 26–35.

——— (1979). *Rape: The Power of Consciousness*. New York: Harper & Row.

Groth, A. Nicholas (1979). *Men Who Rape: The Psychology of the Offender*. New York: Plenum.

Guttmacher, M., and H. Weinhofen (1952). *Psychiatry and the Law*. New York: W. W. Norton.

Hall, Peter M., and John P. Hewitt (1970). "The Quasi-Theory of Communication and the Management of Dissent." *Social Problems*, 18, 17–27.

Halleck, S. (1965). "Emotional Effects of Victimization." In R. Slovenko, ed., *Sexual Behavior and the Law*. Springfield, IL: Charles C Thomas.

Hammer, E., and I. Jacks (1955). "A Study of Rorschach Flexnor and Extensor Human Movements." *Journal of Clinical Psychology*, 11, 63–67.

Hanmer, Jalna, and Mary Maynard (1987). "Introduction: Violence and Gender Stratification." In Jalna Hanmer and Mary Maynard, eds., *Women, Violence and Social Control*. Atlantic Highlands, NJ: Humanities Press International.

Harding, Sandra (1986). *The Science Question in Feminism*. Ithaca, NY: Cornell University Press.

——— (1987). "The Method Question." *Hypatia*, 2, 19–36.

Harding, Sandra, and Jean F. O'Barr, eds. (1987). *Sex and Scientific Inquiry*. Chicago: University of Chicago Press.

Herman, Dianne (1984). "The Rape Culture." In Jo Freeman, ed., *Women: A Feminist Perspective*. Palo Alto, CA: Mayfield.

Herman, Judith (1988). "Considering Sex Offenders." *Signs*, 13, 695–724.

Hernton, Calvin C. (1965). *Sex and Racism in America*. New York: Grove.

Hewitt, John P., and Peter M. Hall (1973). "Social Problems,

Problematic Situations and Quasi-Theories." *American Sociological Review*, 38, 367–74.

Hewitt, John P., and Randall Stokes (1975). "Disclaimers." *American Sociological Review*, 40, 1–11.

Hochschild, Arlie Russell (1975). "The Sociology of Feelings and Emotions: Selected Possibilities." In Marcia Millman and Rosabeth Moss Kantor, eds., *Another Voice*. Garden City, NY: Anchor.

———— (1983). *The Managed Heart: Commercialization of Human Feelings*. Berkeley: University of California Press.

Hoebel, Adamson E. (1954). *The Laws of Primitive Man*. Cambridge, MA: Harvard University Press.

Hollander, B. (1924). *Psychology of Misconduct, Vice and Crime*. New York: Macmillan.

Holmstrom, Lynda Lytle, and Ann Wolbert Burgess (1978a). "Sexual Behavior of Assailant and Victim During Rape." Paper presented at the annual meetings of the American Sociological Association.

———— (1978b). *The Victim of Rape: Institutional Reactions*. New York: John Wiley.

Hooks, Bell (1981). *Ain't I a Woman: Black Women and Feminism*. Boston: South End.

Horney, Karen (1973). "The Problem of Feminine Machochism." In J. Miller, ed., *Psychoanalysis and Women*. New York: Brunner/Mazel.

Hull, Gloria T., Patricia Bell Scott, and Barbara Smith, eds. (1982). *All the Women Are White, All the Blacks Are Men, But Some of Us Are Brave*. Old Westbury, NY: Feminist Press.

Hunt, Morton (1974). *Sexual Behavior in the 1970's*. Chicago: Playboy Press.

Johnson, Allen Griswold (1980). "On the Prevalence of Rape in the United States." *Signs*, 6, 136–46.

Johnson, Stuart, Lorne Gibson, and Rick Linden (1978). "Alcohol and Rape in Winnipeg, 1966–1975." *Journal of Studies on Alcohol*, 39, 1887–94.

Jones, C., and E. Aronson (1973). "Attribution of Fault to a Rape Victim as a Function of Responsibility of the Victim." *Journal of Personality and Social Psychology*, 26, 415–19.

Kanekar, S., and M. Kolsawalla (1977). "Responsibility in Relation to Respectability." *Journal of Social Psychology*, 102, 183–88.

Kanin, E. (1957). "Male Aggression in Dating-Courtship Relations." *American Journal of Sociology*, 63, 197–204.

———— (1965). "Male Sex Aggression and Three Psychiatric Hypotheses." *Journal of Sex Research*, 1, 227–29.

———— (1967). "Reference Groups and Sex Conduct Norm Violation." *Sociological Quarterly*, 8, 495–504.

———— (1969). "Selected Dyadic Aspects of Male Sex Aggression." *Journal of Sex Research*, 5, 12–28.

—— (1970). "Sex Aggression by College Men." *Medical Aspects of Human Sexuality*, September, 28ff.

Karpman, B. (1951). "The Sexual Psychopath." *Journal of Criminal Law and Criminology*, 42, 184–98.

Kelly, Liz (1987). "The Continuum of Sexual Violence." In Jalna Hanmer and Mary Maynard, eds., *Women, Violence, and Social Control*. Atlantic Highlands, NJ: Humanities Press International.

Kerber, Linda K., Catherine G. Greeno, Eleanor E. Maccoby, Zella Luria, Carol B. Stack, and Carol Gilligan (1986). "On *In a Different Voice*: An Interdisciplinary Forum." *Signs*, 11, 304–33.

Kilpatrick, Dean G., Lois Veronen, and Patricia A. Resnick (1979). "The Aftermath of Rape: Recent Empirical Findings." *American Journal of Orthopsychiatry*, 49, 658–69.

Kirkpatrick, C., and E. Kanin (1957). "Male Sex Aggression on a University Campus." *American Sociological Review*, 22, 52–58.

Knight, Raymond A., Ruth Rosenberg, and Beth Schneider (1985). "Classification of Sexual Offenders: Perspectives, Methods and Validation." In Ann Wolbert Burgess, ed., *Rape and Sexual Assault: A Research Handbook*. New York: Garland.

Koss, Mary P., Christine A. Gidycz, and Nadine Wisniewski (1987). "The Scope of Rape: Incidence and Prevalence of Sexual Aggression and Victimization in a National Sample of Students in Higher Education." *Journal of Consulting and Clinical Psychology*, 55, 162–70.

Koss, Mary P., and Kenneth E. Leonard (1984). "Sexually Aggressive Men: Empirical Findings and Theoretical Implications." In Neil Malamuth and Edward Donnerstein, eds., *Pornography and Sexual Aggression*. New York: Academic Press.

Koss, Mary P., Kenneth E. Leonard, Dana A. Beezley, and Cheryl J. Oros (1985). "Nonstranger Sexual Aggression: A Discriminant Analysis of the Psychological Characteristics of Undetected Offenders." *Sex Roles*, 12, 981–92.

Krulewitz, J., and E. Payne (1978). "Attributions About Rape: Effects of Rapist Force, Observer Sex, and Sex Role Attitudes." *Journal of Applied Social Psychology*, 8, 291–305.

Kutchinsky, B. (1971). "Toward an Exploration of the Decrease in Registered Sex Crimes in Copenhagen." In *Technical Reports of the Commission on Obscenity and Pornography*, Vol. 7. Washington DC: Government Printing Office.

LaFree, Gary D. (1980). "The Effect of Sexual Stratification by Race on Official Reactions to Rape." *American Sociological Review*, 45, 824–54.

—— (1982). "Male Power and Female Victimization: Towards a Theory of Interracial Rape." *American Journal of Sociology*, 88, 311–28.

—— (1989). *Rape and Criminal Justice: The Social Construction of Sexual Assault*. Belmont, CA: Wadsworth.

LaFree, Gary D., Barbara F. Reskin, and Christy A. Visher (1985). "Jurors' Reactions to Victims' Behavior and Legal Issues in Sexual Assault Trials." *Social Problems*, 32, 389–406.

Lang, Alan R., Daniel J. Goeckner, Vincent J. Adesso, and G. Alan Marlatt (1975). "Effects of Alcohol on Aggression in Male Social Drinkers." *Journal of Abnormal Psychology*, 84, 508–18.

Langevin, Ron, Daniel Paitich, and Anne E. Russon (1985). "Are Rapists Sexually Anomalous, Aggressive or Both?" In Ron Langevin, ed., *Erotic Preference, Gender Identity, and Aggression in Men: New Research Studies*. Hillsdale, NJ: Lawrence Erlbaum.

Lauer, Robert H., and Linda Boardman (1971). "Role-Taking: Theory, Typology, and Propositions." *Sociology and Social Research*, 55, 137–48.

Law Enforcement Assistance Administration (1974). *Crime in the Nation's Five Largest Cities*. Washington, DC: U.S. Department of Justice, National Criminal Justice Information and Statistics Service.

——— (1978). *Newsletter*, September.

Laws, D., and M. Holman (1978). "Sexual Response Faking by Pedophiles." *Criminal Justice and Behavior*, 5, 343–56.

LeGrand, Camille (1973). "Rape and Rape Laws: Sexism in Society and Law." *California Law Review*, 61, 919–43.

Linz, Daniel, Edward Donnerstein, and Steven Penrod (1984). "The Effects of Multiple Exposure to Filmed Violence Against Women." *Journal of Communication*, Summer, 130–47.

Lipman-Blumen, Jean (1984). *Gender Roles and Power*. Englewood Cliffs, NJ: Prentice-Hall.

Littner, Ner (1973). "Psychology of the Sex Offender: Causes, Treatment, Prognosis." *Police Law Quarterly*, 3, 5–31.

Lizotte, Alan J. (1986). "Determinants of Completing Rape and Assault." *Journal of Quantitative Criminology*, 2, 203–17.

Llewellyn, Karl N., and E. Adamson Hoebel (1941). *The Cheyenne Way: Conflict and Case Law in Primitive Jurisprudence*. Norman: University of Oklahoma Press.

Luckenbill, David (1977). "Criminal Homicide as a Situated Transaction." *Social Problems*, 25, 176–87.

Lystad, Mary Hanemann (1985). "The National Center for the Prevention and Control of Rape: A Federal Research Agenda." In Ann Wolbert Burgess, ed., *Rape and Sexual Assault: A Research Handbook*. New York: Garland.

MacAndrew, Craig, and Robert B. Edgerton (1969). *Drunken Comportment: A Social Explanation*. Chicago: Aldine.

MacKinnon, Catherine A. (1983). "Feminism, Marxism, Method, and the State: Toward Feminist Jurisprudence." *Signs*, 8, 635–59.

——— (1987). *Feminism Unmodified: Discourses on Life and Law*. Cambridge, MA: Harvard University Press.

Malamuth, Neil M. (1981a). "Aggression Against Women: Cultural and Individual Causes." In Neil M. Malamuth and Edward

Donnerstein eds., *Pornography and Sexual Aggression*. New York: Academic Press.

—— (1981b). "Rape Fantasies as a Function of Exposure to Violent Sexual Stimuli." *Archives of Sexual Behavior*, 10, 33–47.

—— (1983). "Factors Associated with Rape as Predictors of Laboratory Aggression Against Women." *Journal of Personality and Social Psychology*, 45, 432–42.

Malamuth, Neil M., and John Briere (1986). "Sexual Violence in the Media: Indirect Effects on Aggression Against Women." *Journal of Social Issues*, 42, 75–92.

Malamuth, Neil M., and James V. P. Check (1981). "The Effect of Mass Media Exposure on Acceptance of Violence Against Women: A Field Experiment." *Journal of Research in Personality*, 15, 435–46.

—— (1983). "Sexual Arousal to Rape Depictions: Individual Differences." *Journal of Abnormal Psychology*, 92, 55–67.

—— (1985). "The Effects of Aggressive Pornography on Beliefs in Rape Myths: Individual Differences." *Journal of Research in Personality*, 19, 299–320.

Malamuth, Neil M., James V. P. Check and John Briere (1986). "Sexual Arousal in Response to Aggression: Ideological, Aggressive, and Sexual Correlates." *Journal of Personality and Social Psychology*, 50, 330–39.

Malamuth, Neil M., Scott Haber, and Seymour Feshbach (1980). "Testing Hypotheses Regarding Rape: Exposure to Sexual Violence, Sex Difference, and the 'Normality' of Rapists." *Journal of Research in Personality*, 14, 121–37.

Malamuth, Neil M., Maggie Heim, and Seymour Feshbach (1980). "Sexual Responsiveness of College Students to Rape Depictions: Inhibitory and Disinhibitory Effects." *Journal of Personality and Social Psychology*, 38, 399–408.

Malamuth, Neil M., and Barry Spinner (1980). "A Longitudinal Content Analysis of Sexual Violence in the Best-Selling Erotic Magazines." *Journal of Sex Research*, 16, 226–37.

Mandelbaum, David G. (1965). "Alcohol and Culture." *Current Anthropology*, 6, 281–93.

Marolla, Joseph, and Diana Scully (1986). "Attitudes Toward Women, Violence, and Rape: A Comparison of Convicted Rapists and Other Felons." *Deviant Behavior*, 7, 337–55.

Martin, Patricia Yaney, and Robert A. Hummer (1989). "Fraternities and Rape on Campus." *Gender and Society*, 3, 457–73.

McCaghy, Charles H. (1968). "Drinking and Deviance Disavowal: The Case of Child Molesters." *Social Problems*, 16, 43–49.

Medea, Andrea, and Kathleen Thompsoon (1974). *Against Rape*. New York: Farrar, Straus, & Giroux.

Mills, C. Wright (1940). "Situated Actions and Vocabularies of Motive." *American Sociological Review*, 5, 904–13.

Millsaps, Bill (1988). "Even Legends Can Make Spectacular Blunders." *Richmond* (VA) *Times-Dispatch*, May 4, D1.

Nelson, Steven, and Menachem Amir (1975). "The Hitchhike Victim of Rape: A Research Report." In Israel Drapkin and Emilio Viano, eds., *Victimology: A New Focus*. Lexington, MA: Lexington.

O'Kelly, Charlotte G., and Larry S. Carney (1986). *Women and Men in Society*. Belmont, CA: Wadsworth.

Parsons, Talcott (1947). "Certain Primary Sources and Patterns of Aggression in the Social Structure of the Western World." *Psychiatry*, 10, 167–81.

Pietropinto, Anthony, and Jacqueline Simenauer (1977). *Beyond the Male Myth*. New York: Times Books.

Pleck, Joseph (1981). *The Myth of Masculinity*. Cambridge: MIT Press.

Ploscowe, Morris (1968). "Rape." In Edward Sagarin and Donald MacNamara, eds., *Problems of Sexual Behavior*. New York: Thomas Crowell.

Queen's Bench Foundation (1976). *Rape: Prevention and Resistance*. San Francisco: Author.

——— (1978). "The Rapist and His Crime." In L. Savitz and N. Johnston, eds., *Crime in Society*. New York: John Wiley.

Quinsey, Vernon L., and Douglas Upfold (1985). "Rape Completion and Victim Injury as a Function of Female Resistance Strategy." *Canadian Journal of Behavioral Science*, 17, 40–50.

Rada, Richard, ed. (1978). *Clinical Aspects of the Rapist*. New York: Grune & Stratton.

Riger, Stephanie, and Margaret T. Gordon (1981). "The Fear of Rape: A Study in Social Control." *Journal of Social Issues*, 37, 71–92.

Ruch, Libby O., Susan Meyer Chandler, and Richard A. Harter (1980). "Life Change and Rape Impact." *Journal of Health and Social Behavior*, 21, 248–60.

Rumenik, D., D. Capasso, and C. Hendrick (1977). "Experimenter Sex Effects in Behavioral Research." *Psychological Bulletin*, 84, 852–77.

Russell, Diana E. H. (1975). *The Politics of Rape*. New York: Stein & Day.

——— (1982). "The Prevalence and Incidence of Forcible Rape and Attempted Rape of Females." *Victimology: An International Journal*, 7, 81–93.

Russell, Diana E. H., and Nancy Howell (1983). "The Prevalence of Rape in the United States Revisited." *Signs*, 8, 688–95.

Sagarin, E. (1976). "Prison Homosexuality and Its Effects on Post-Prison Sexual Behavior." *Psychiatry*, 39, 245–57.

Sanday, Peggy Reeves (1979). *The Socio-Cultural Context of Rape*. Washington, DC: U.S. Department of Commerce, National Technical Information Services.

Schlenker, Barry R., and Bruce W. Darby (1981). "The Use of Apologies in Social Predicaments." *Social Psychology Quarterly*, 44, 271–78.

Schwendinger, Julia A., and Herman Schwendinger (1983). *Rape and Inequality*. Beverly Hills, CA: Sage.

Scott, Marvin, and Stanford Lyman (1968). "Accounts." *American Sociological Review*, 33, 46–62.

Scully, Diana (1980). *Men Who Control Women's Health*. Boston: Houghton Mifflin.

—— (1988). "Convicted Rapists' Perceptions of Self and Victim: Role Taking and Emotions." *Gender and Society*, 2, 200–13.

Scully, Diana, and Pauline Bart (1973). "A Funny Thing Happened on the Way to the Orifice: Women in Gynecology Texts." *American Journal of Sociology*, 78, 1045–51.

Scully, Diana, and Joseph Marolla (1984). "Convicted Rapists' Vocabulary of Motive: Excuses and Justifications." *Social Problems*, 31, 530–44.

—— (1985a). "Rape and Psychiatric Vocabularies of Motive: Alternative Perspectives." In Ann Wolbert Burgess, ed., *Rape and Sexual Assault: A Research Handbook*. New York: Garland.

—— (1985b). "'Riding the Bull at Gilley's': Convicted Rapists Describe the Rewards of Rape." *Social Problems*, 32, 251–63.

Sherma, Julia, and Evelyn Beck, eds. (1979). *The Prism of Sex: Essays in the Sociology of Knowledge*. Madison: University of Wisconsin Press.

Shields, William M., and Lea M. Shields (1983). "Forcible Rape: An Evolutionary Perspective." *Ethology and Sociobiology*, 4, 115–36.

Shore, Barbara K. (1979). *An Examination of Critical Process and Outcome Factors in Rape*. Rockville, MD: National Institute of Mental Health.

Shott, Susan (1979). "Emotions and Social Life: A Symbolic Interactionist Analysis." *American Journal of Sociology*, 84, 1317–34.

Silverman, Ira (1970). "Compulsive Masculinity and Delinquency." Unpublished dissertation, Ohio State University.

Silverman, Ira, and S. Dinitz (1974). "Compulsive Masculinity and Delinquency: An Empirical Investigation." *Criminology*, 11, 498–515.

Simon, Jesse, and Jack Zusman (1983). "The Effect of Contextual Factors on Psychiatrists' Perception of Illness: A Case Study." *Journal of Health and Social Behavior*, 24, 186–98.

Slade, Joseph W. (1984). "Violence in the Hard-Core Pornographic Film: A Historical Survey." *Journal of Communication*, Summer, 148–63.

Smith, Don D. (1976). "The Social Content of Pornography." *Journal of Communication*, Winter, 16–24.

Smith, Dorothy (1974). "Women's Perspective as a Radical Critique of Sociology." *Sociological Inquiry*, 44, 7–13.

—— (1979). "A Sociology for Women." In Julia A. Sherma and Evelyn Beck, eds., *The Prism of Sex: Essays in the Sociology of Knowledge*. Madison: University of Wisconsin Press.

Smithyman, Samuel (1978). "The Undetected Rapist." Unpublished dissertation, Claremont Graduate School.

Spence, J., R. Helmreich, and J. Stapp (1973). "A Short Version of the Attitudes Toward Women Scale (AWS)." *Bulletin of the Psychonomic Society*, 2, 219–20.

Stacey, Judith, and Barrie Thorne (1985). "The Missing Feminist Revolution in Sociology." *Social Problems*, 32, 301–16.

Stanko, Elizabeth A. (1985). *Intimate Intrusions: Women's Experience of Male Violence*. New York: Routledge & Kegan Paul.

Stokes, Randall, and John P. Hewitt (1976). "Aligning Actions." *American Sociological Review*, 41, 838–49.

Sykes, Gresham M., and David Matza (1957). "Techniques of Neutralization." *American Sociological Review*, 22, 667–69.

Thomas, Darwin, David D. Franks, and James M. Calonico (1972). "Role-Taking and Power in Social Psychology." *American Journal of Sociology*, 37, 605–14.

Thore, F., and T. Haupt (1966). "The Objective Measurement of Sex Attitudes and Behavior in Adult Males." *Journal of Clinical Psychology*, 22, 395–403.

Thornhill, Randy, and Nancy Wilmsen Thornhill (1983). "Human Rape: An Evolutionary Analysis." *Ethology and Sociobiology*, 4, 137–73.

Tieger, Todd (1981). "Self-Rated Likelihood of Raping and Social Perception of Rape." *Journal of Research in Personality*, 15, 147–58.

Turner, Ralph (1962). "Role-Taking: Process Versus Conformity." In A. Rose, ed., *Human Behavior and Social Process*. Boston: Houghton Mifflin.

von Hentig, Hans (1940). "Remarks on the Interaction of Perpetrator and Victim." *Journal of Criminal Law and Criminology*, 31, 303–9.

Warr, Mark (1985). "Fear of Rape Among Urban Women." *Social Problems*, 32, 238–50.

Weis, Kurt, and Sandra Borges (1973). "Victimology and Rape: The Case of the Legitimate Victim." *Issues in Criminology*, 8, 71–115.

Weiss, J., E. Rogers, M. Darwin, and C. Dutton (1955). "A Study of Girl Sex Offenders." *Psychiatric Quarterly*, 29, 1–29.

Welsh, Patrick (1988). "Drink and Drugs: Have Our Colleges Lost Control?" *Washington Post*, November 6.

West, Donald J. (1983). "Sex Offenses and Offending." In Michael Tonry and Norval Morris, eds., *Crime and Justice: An Annual Review of Research*. Chicago: University of Chicago Press.

Williams, Joyce (1978). "Good Victims and Real Rapes: A Comparison of Anglo, Black, and Mexican American Perspective." Paper presented at the annual meetings of the Southwestern Sociological Association, Houston.

——— (1979). "Sex Role Stereotypes, Women's Liberation and Rape: A Cross-Cultural Analysis of Attitudes." *Sociological Symposium*, Winter, 61–97.

Williams, Linda S. (1984). "The Classic Rape: When Do Victims Report?" *Social Problems*, 31, 459–67.

Wilson, G. Terence (1977). "Alcohol and Human Sexual Behavior." *Behavioral Research and Therapy*, 15, 239–52.

Wilson, G. Terence, and David M. Lawson (1976). "Expectancies, Alcohol, and Sexual Arousal in Male Social Drinkers." *Journal of Abnormal Psychology*, 85, 587–94.

Zillman, Dolf, and Jennings Bryant (1982). "Pornography, Sexual Callousness, and the Trivialization of Rape." *Journal of Communication*, Autumn, 10–21.

Zinn, Maxine Baca (1982). "Mexican-American Women in the Social Sciences." *Signs*, 8, 259–72.

About the Author

Diana Scully is associate professor of sociology and coordinator of the Women's Studies Program at Virginia Commonwealth University, and the author of *Men Who Control Women's Health* (1980).

Index